GAME CHANGERS WRITING THE E-SPORTS SUCCESS STORY

Game Changers Writing The E-sports Success Story

RAFEAL MECHLORE

UNIEK ENTERPRISES

CONTENTS

INDEX

Introduction

The development and fast rising of esports lately have been downright a peculiarity. What was once a specialty subculture has changed into a worldwide diversion force to be reckoned with, with a great many fans, billions of dollars in income, and a developing rundown of whiz players and groups. The example of overcoming adversity of esports is an intriguing story of development, enthusiasm, and the consistently changing scene of the computerized age. In this article, we will investigate the variables and people that play played significant parts in molding the esports biological system and making it one of the most thrilling and worthwhile types of diversion in the 21st hundred years.

Esports, short for electronic games, alludes to serious video gaming, where players or groups go head to head in different computer game titles, frequently for significant monetary rewards and distinction. While cutthroat gaming has been around for a really long time, the new blast in its prevalence is a somewhat late turn of events, energized by propels in innovation, the ascent of streaming stages like Jerk, and the production of coordinated associations and competitions.

One of the critical major advantages in the esports example of overcoming adversity is the development of innovation. The fast progression of equipment and programming has essentially added to the development of esports. In the beginning of cutthroat gaming, players frequently needed to accumulate in little, nearby arcades to contend. These early contests were restricted by the accessible innovation, with most games being played on maturing, coin-worked machines. Nonetheless, as home gaming control center and PCs turned out to be all the more remarkable, the potential for cutthroat gaming developed.

The change to internet gaming was a crucial second. With the approach of the web, players could rival others from around the world, separating topographical boundaries and extending the potential player pool. Games like "Tremor" and "StarCraft" were among the trailblazers of online serious gaming, and their prosperity established the groundwork for what was to come.

The ascent of streaming stages, for example, Jerk, denoted another significant defining moment in the esports business. Streaming permitted players and expert gamers to communicate their ongoing interaction to a worldwide crowd, leading to another age of esports VIPs. Watchers could watch their number one players in real life, gain from their procedures, and even communicate with them continuously through talk. This immediate commitment among players and fans was a unique advantage, as it made a more private and close association, something customary games attempted to accomplish.

Proficient gaming associations and the coming of esports associations assumed a basic part in the business' development. Associations like Fnatic, Group Fluid, and SK Telecom T1 furnished players with monetary help as well as legitimized esports as a lifelong decision. These associations marked players, gave them assets and preparing offices, and contended in different associations and competitions. The steadiness and construction these associations brought to esports were instrumental in drawing in top ability and developing the fan base.

One of the most remarkable esports examples of overcoming adversity is the ascent of South Korea as a worldwide force to be reckoned with in cutthroat gaming. South Korea has created a portion of the world's most prevailing players and groups in games like "StarCraft," "Class of Legends," and "Overwatch." This predominance can be credited to a few variables, including serious areas of strength for a culture, foundation, and government support. In South Korea, esports players are dealt with like superstars, with their matches broadcast on public TV and worthwhile sponsorship bargains. The Korean model of esports achievement has been a plan for different locales hoping to lay out their presence in the business.

The internationalization of esports has been one more key calculate its development. As esports spread to various regions of the planet, it made a worldwide local area of players and fans. Significant worldwide competitions, similar to The Worldwide for "Dota 2" and the Class of Legends Big showdown, pulled in groups and crowds from all sides of the globe. The globalization of esports extended the player base as well as enhanced the business' ability pool, making it more serious and interesting to a more extensive crowd.

Esports additionally drew motivation from conventional games, embracing components, for example, diversifying, organized associations, and normalized rules. The presentation of establishment frameworks in associations like the Overwatch Association and the Class of Legends Title Series (LCS) reflected the model of pro athletics associations like the NBA and NFL. Diversifying carried monetary soundness to the esports biological system by permitting group proprietors to put resources into a drawn out future with a reliable spot in the association.

Organized associations and normalized rules added a layer of impressive skill to esports. Rather than an assortment of dissipated competitions, many games currently have laid out associations with normal seasons and end of the season games. This configuration not just given a more dependable timetable to fans yet additionally pulled in customary games associations like the New York Yankees and the Dallas Ranchers, who saw the capability of esports and put vigorously in it.

Besides, colleges and schools started offering esports grants, perceiving the capability of esports as a reasonable profession way for youthful gifts. University esports associations have developed considerably, further legitimizing serious gaming as a way to training and vocation open doors. The acknowledgment of esports as a real field of study and profession choice has been a huge move toward the business' example of overcoming adversity.

Esports owes quite a bit of its prosperity to an enthusiastic and connected with local area of fans. These fans have been instrumental in driving the business forward, from grassroots occasions to enormous worldwide competitions. Esports occasions consistently fill fields and arenas, with millions more watching on the web. The enthusiastic fan base has gotten sponsorships, broadcasting arrangements, and financial backers, further powering the business' development.

Game distributers likewise assumed a vital part in the esports example of overcoming adversity. Organizations like Uproar Games, Snowstorm Diversion, and Valve not just fostered the games that filled in as the establishment for serious gaming yet additionally effectively upheld and advanced the esports scenes encompassing their titles. They coordinated competitions, offered monetary help, and persistently adjusted and refreshed their games to guarantee a fair and serious climate.

The ascent of expert players as VIPs denoted one more defining moment in the esports business. Gamers like Faker in "Class of Legends," s1mple in "Counter-Strike: Worldwide Hostile," and Ninja in "Fortnite" have become commonly recognized names, rising above the gaming scene and showing up in traditional press. These players, with their remarkable abilities and drawing in characters, have drawn in fans past the gaming local area and brought esports into the standard.

Notwithstanding players, committed esports reporters and experts, frequently alluded to as casters, play had a huge impact in the business' prosperity. Casters give in depth discourse, examination, and amusement during esports communicates, assisting watchers with grasping the subtleties of the game and building energy. A significant number of them have become as notorious as the actual players, assisting with forming the story of esports contests and make essential minutes.

The esports biological system has likewise been advanced by satisfied makers and forces to be reckoned with. YouTube and Jerk characters who transfer games, make directs, and engage their crowds play had an imperative impact in advancing esports titles. Content makers like PewDiePie, Cover, and Pokimane have a large number of endorsers and watchers, and their help has been instrumental in promoting games and esports associations.

Esports occasions themselves have additionally been changed into stupendous creations. With huge fields, elaborate stage plans, and expert telecom, esports competitions have arrived at a degree of creation quality that rivals customary games. The Global, for instance, is known for its luxurious opening functions, and the Class of Legends Big showdown has sold out major arenas.

The financial aspects of esports have become progressively intricate, with different income streams adding to the business' prosperity. Sponsorships from organizations like Intel, Coca-Cola, and Mercedes-Benz have infused significant financing into esports occasions and groups. Promoting and broadcasting manages stages like Jerk and YouTube have likewise assumed a huge part in producing income. The Overwatch Association marked a long term telecom manage YouTube, while Jerk stays a predominant stage for streaming esports content.

Promoting is one more rewarding road for esports. Groups and associations sell shirts, covers, and other product, and fans are anxious to help their number one groups and players by buying these things. Virtual products, like in-game skins and things, have likewise turned into a significant wellspring of income. Games like "Fortnite" and "Counter-Strike: Worldwide Hostile" permit players to buy corrective things, and a part of the returns frequently goes toward subsidizing esports competitions and prize pools.

The ascent of esports wagering has added one more layer of monetary help to the business. Esports wagering stages have filled in ubiquity, permitting fans to bet on the results of matches and competitions. The flood of wagering cash has expanded the stakes and energy of esports contests, while likewise giving extra income streams to the business.

As of late, blockchain innovation and non-fungible tokens (NFTs) have advanced into esports, offering new open doors for fans and players. Blockchain takes into account .

1. **The emergence of e-sports as a global phenomenon**

   The development of esports as a worldwide peculiarity has been completely exceptional. What started as a specialty subculture inside the universe of video gaming has changed into a monstrous industry, attracting a huge number of fans, creating billions of dollars in income, and catapulting proficient players and groups to superstardom. The example of overcoming adversity of esports is a demonstration of the force of development, innovation, and the consistently advancing scene of the computerized age.

   Esports, an abbreviated type of "electronic games," alludes to serious video gaming where players or groups contend in different computer game titles, frequently for significant monetary rewards, acknowledgment, and a committed fan base. While serious gaming has existed in different structures for a really long time, the touchy development and acknowledgment of esports as a genuine type of diversion and contest is a later turn of events. It has been driven by a mix of elements, remembering progressions for innovation, the ascent of streaming stages, and the foundation of coordinated associations and competitions.

   One of the vital major advantages in the esports example of overcoming adversity is the advancement of innovation. The fast advancement of equipment

and programming plays had a critical impact in the development of esports. In the beginning of cutthroat gaming, players frequently accumulated in neighborhood arcades to contend. These early rivalries were
restricted by the accessible innovation, with most games being played on maturing, coin-worked machines. In any case, as home gaming control center and PCs turned out to be all the more impressive, the potential for serious gaming developed dramatically.

The change to web based gaming denoted an essential crossroads in the historical backdrop of esports. With the appearance of the web, players could rival others from around the world, separating geological boundaries and extending the potential player pool. Games like "Shudder" and "StarCraft" were among the trailblazers of online cutthroat gaming, and their prosperity established the groundwork for what was to come.

The ascent of streaming stages, especially Jerk, denoted another critical defining moment in the esports business. Streaming permitted proficient gamers to communicate their ongoing interaction to a worldwide crowd, leading to another age of esports big names. Watchers could watch their number one players in real life, gain from their systems, and even cooperate with them continuously through talk. This immediate commitment among players and fans was a unique advantage, as it made a more private and personal association, something that conventional games had attempted to accomplish.

Proficient gaming associations and the foundation of esports associations assumed a vital part in the business' development. Associations like Fnatic, Group Fluid, and SK Telecom T1 offered monetary help to players as well as legitimized esports as a practical vocation decision. These associations marked players, offered assets, and preparing offices, and contended in different associations and competitions. The solidness and design these associations brought to esports were instrumental in drawing in top ability and developing the fan base.

One of the most convincing examples of overcoming adversity in esports is the ascent of South Korea as a worldwide force to be reckoned with in cutthroat gaming. South Korea has created a portion of the world's most prevailing players and groups in games like "StarCraft," "Class of Legends," and "Overwatch." This predominance can be credited to a few variables, including areas of strength for a culture, foundation, and government support. In South Korea, esports players are dealt with like VIPs, with their matches broadcast on public TV and worthwhile sponsorship bargains. The Korean model of esports achievement has filled in as a plan for different locales hoping to lay out their presence in the business.

The internationalization of esports has been one more key figure its development. As esports spread to various regions of the planet, it made a worldwide local area of players and fans. Significant worldwide competitions, for example, The Worldwide for "Dota 2" and the Class of Legends Big showdown, pulled in groups and crowds from all sides of the globe. The globalization of esports extended the player base as well as broadened the business' ability pool, making it more serious and interesting to a more extensive crowd.

Esports likewise drew motivation from customary games, embracing components, for example, diversifying, organized associations, and normalized rules. The presentation of establishment frameworks in associations like the Overwatch Association and the Class of Legends Title Series (LCS) reflected the model of elite athletics associations like the NBA and NFL. Diversifying carried monetary steadiness to the esports biological system by permitting group proprietors to put resources into a drawn out future with a reliable spot in the association.

Organized associations and normalized rules added a layer of impressive skill to esports. Rather than an assortment of dispersed competitions, many games currently have laid out associations with customary seasons and end of the season games. This configuration not just given a more solid timetable to fans yet in addition pulled in customary games associations like the New York Yankees and the Dallas Ranchers, who saw the capability of esports and put vigorously in it.

Moreover, colleges and universities started offering esports grants, perceiving the capability of esports as a practical vocation way for youthful gifts. University esports associations have developed significantly, further legitimizing serious gaming as a way to instruction and vocation valuable open doors. The acknowledgment of esports as a genuine field of study and profession choice has been a huge move toward the business' example of overcoming adversity.

Esports owes a lot of its prosperity to an energetic and connected with local area of fans. These fans have been instrumental in driving the business forward, from grassroots occasions to enormous worldwide competitions. Esports occasions consistently fill fields and arenas, with millions more watching on the web. The enthusiastic fan base has gotten sponsorships, broadcasting arrangements, and ventures, further powering the business' development.

Game distributers likewise assumed a urgent part in the esports example of overcoming adversity. Organizations like Mob Games, Snowstorm Diversion, and Valve not just fostered the games that filled in as the establishment for serious gaming yet in addition effectively upheld and advanced the esports scenes encompassing their titles. They coordinated competitions, offered monetary help, and consistently adjusted and refreshed their games to guarantee a fair and cutthroat climate.

The ascent of expert players as superstars denoted one more defining moment in the esports business. Gamers like Faker in "Class of Legends," s1mple in "Counter-Strike: Worldwide Hostile," and Ninja in "Fortnite" have become easily recognized names, rising above the gaming scene and showing up in traditional press. These players, with their extraordinary abilities and drawing in characters, have drawn in fans past the gaming local area and brought esports into the standard.

Notwithstanding players, devoted esports pundits and examiners, frequently alluded to as casters, play had a critical impact in the business' prosperity. Casters give in depth discourse, examination, and amusement during esports communicates, assisting watchers with grasping the subtleties of the game and building fervor. A significant number of them have become as notable as the actual players, forming the story of esports contests and making noteworthy minutes.

The esports environment has likewise been enhanced by happy makers and powerhouses. YouTube and Jerk characters who transfer games, make directs, and engage their crowds play had a crucial impact in advancing esports titles. Content makers like PewDiePie, Cover, and Pokimane have a great many endorsers and watchers, and their help has been instrumental in promoting games and esports associations.

Esports occasions themselves have been changed into tremendous creations. With huge fields, elaborate stage plans, and expert telecom, esports competitions have arrived at a degree of creation quality that rivals customary games. The Global, for instance, is known for its extreme opening functions, and the Class of Legends Big showdown has sold out major arenas.

The financial matters of esports have become progressively mind boggling, with different income streams adding to the business' prosperity. Sponsorships from organizations like Intel, Coca-Cola, and Mercedes-Benz have infused significant subsidizing into esports occasions and groups. Publicizing and broadcasting manages stages like Jerk and YouTube have additionally assumed a critical part in producing income.

2. **Purpose and scope of the book**

The reason and extent of this book are to dig profound into the multi-layered universe of esports, investigating its starting points, development, and the different variables that have added to its ascent as a worldwide peculiarity. Esports, a term got from "electronic games," addresses cutthroat video gaming where players or groups take part in straight on fights in different computer game titles, frequently with significant awards and developing fan bases. The excursion of esports, from its unassuming starting points to its ongoing status, is an intriguing story of development, innovation, enthusiasm, and local area.

Esports, when considered a specialty hobby inside the more extensive domain of video gaming, has arisen as a strong social and monetary power lately. The business' quick rising has prompted various inquiries and conversations about its importance, its position in the diversion scene, and its true capacity for what's to come. This book means to give a thorough investigation of these subjects, revealing insight into the past, present, and future of esports.

One of the essential targets of this book is to follow the authentic development of esports. Understanding where everything started is fundamental to see the value in how far the business has come. We'll analyze the underlying foundations of serious gaming, from early arcade rivalries to the ascent of LAN parties and the approach of web based gaming. Thusly, we can observe the structure obstructs that prepared for esports to turn into a worldwide peculiarity.

Besides, this book will investigate the job of innovation as a unique advantage in the esports story. Headways in gaming equipment, the ascent of strong gaming control center and PCs, and the advancement of high velocity web associations generally assumed significant parts in forming esports. The book will dig into the mechanical achievements that altered the business and gave the foundation to proficient cutthroat gaming.

Streaming stages like Jerk and the ascent of online substance creation are additionally key parts of the esports story. The immediate communication among players and fans, made conceivable through live streaming, denoted a critical change in how esports is consumed and experienced. The book will dig into the effect of streaming and the rise of esports big names who have drawn in worldwide followings.

One more crucial part of the book's extension is the investigation of expert gaming associations and the foundation of esports associations. Proficient groups and associations have added a layer of design, association, and authenticity to the business. These elements have led to the vocations of expert players, gave them assets and backing, and transformed esports into a worthwhile profession choice. We will inspect the commitments of associations and the manners in which they have molded the cutthroat scene.

Besides, the book will investigate the worldwide reach of esports. The business' development to different regions of the planet has made an assorted local area of players and fans. Worldwide competitions have drawn groups and crowds from everywhere the globe, stressing the worldwide idea of cutthroat gaming. We will investigate the worldwide peculiarities of esports and how it has risen above boundaries and societies.

Esports' reception of components from conventional games, including diversifying, organized associations, and normalized rules, is one more critical part of the book's extension. We will dig into how these components have added a layer of incredible skill and commonality to the business. Diversifying, specifically, has carried monetary strength to esports and pulled in speculations from conventional games associations.

The book will likewise address the instructive part of esports. The development of university esports associations and grants for capable players means the business' acknowledgment as a genuine field of study and vocation decision. We'll investigate the job of schooling and the way things are forming the up and coming age of esports experts.

A focal subject of this book is the enthusiastic and drawn in local area of esports fans. Their devotion, backing, and excitement play had a huge impact in the business' development. We will examine the significance of the fan base, from grassroots occasions to gigantic worldwide competitions, and the effect it has had on the business' monetary supportability.

The book will likewise focus on the assembly of esports with conventional games. The inclusion of conventional games associations, proficient competitors, and the joining of esports into customary games has made a remarkable cooperative energy between the two universes. We will investigate how this cooperative energy is reshaping the scene of both esports and conventional games.

As the esports business keeps on developing, it faces its reasonable part of difficulties, and the book won't avoid resolving these issues. Concerns, for example, player burnout, match-fixing, and orientation variety are fundamental themes for conversation. The book will look at how the business is handling these difficulties and endeavoring to keep up with its honesty and inclusivity.

The book will likewise dig into the monetary parts of esports. Sponsorships, promoting, broadcasting arrangements, marketing, and the ascent of esports wagering have all added to the business' monetary achievement. We will investigate these income streams and how they have formed the business' monetary scene.

Lately, advancements, for example, blockchain innovation and non-fungible tokens (NFTs) have advanced into esports, offering new open doors for fans and players. These advancements can possibly reform how esports content is adapted and shared, and the book will give bits of knowledge into these turns of events.

The last section of this book will plan ahead for esports. We will investigate the potential bearings the business might take, from the combination of computer generated reality and increased reality advances to the effect of 5G organizations on the streaming quality and availability of esports content. The connection among esports and conventional games, government acknowledgment and backing, and the always developing cutthroat scene will likewise be areas of concentration as we peer into the future of esports.

The esports example of overcoming adversity is a demonstration of human development, flexibility, and the unfathomable capability of the computerized age. Which began as a specialty side interest has developed into a worldwide peculiarity, drawing in speculation, sponsorship, and consideration from all edges of the world. Esports have risen above social, geological, and generational limits, uniting a large number of energetic fans and setting out vocation open doors for players, content makers, and experts in the business.

This book looks to exemplify the unprecedented excursion of esports, from its starting points to its current state, and to give experiences into the valuable open doors and difficulties that lie ahead. The tale of esports is a unique story that proceeds to unfurl, and this book means to catch its pith, investigating the complex universe of serious gaming and its consistently extending job in the worldwide media outlet.

Chapter 1

The Genesis of E-sports

The beginning of esports is a story profoundly entwined with the development of video gaming itself. To comprehend the foundations of this worldwide peculiarity, we should travel back to when computer games were still in their earliest stages, and the idea of expert serious gaming was nevertheless a flicker not too far off. As we investigate the beginning of cutthroat gaming, we'll uncover the starting points of esports, the crucial job of innovation, and the development of an energetic local area that established the groundwork for the business we know today.

Computer games, the basic structure blocks of esports, appeared during the mid-twentieth 100 years. Everything started with the improvement of "Tennis for Two" in 1958, a basic tennis recreation game made by physicist William Higinbotham on an oscilloscope show. This simple creation can be viewed as one of the earliest types of video gaming, and it laid the basis for the advanced amusement we appreciate today.

The resulting many years saw the introduction of different gaming achievements, including "Pong" in 1972 and "Space Trespassers" in 1978. These games denoted the early ubiquity of arcades and home gaming consoles, offering a brief look at the potential for serious gaming.

The rise of arcades, where people could assemble to play computer games, was an essential turn of events. Arcades united players from various foundations to contend in games like "Pac-Man," "Jackass Kong," and "Road Warrior." These early rivalries, while casual, planted the seeds of cutthroat gaming by giving a stage to players to exhibit their abilities.

The 1980s saw the ascent of the first perceived esports occasion, the "Space Trespassers Title" coordinated by Atari. This noteworthy contest pulled in north of 10,000 members, exhibiting the developing interest in cutthroat gaming. While the awards were humble, the occasion offered a sample of what was conceivable, and it filled in as a forerunner to the coordinated esports competitions we have today.

All the while, the appearance of home gaming consoles like the Atari 2600 and the Nintendo Theater setup (NES) started to rethink how computer games were played. These control center permitted players to encounter the excitement of gaming in the solace of their own homes, establishing the groundwork for a blossoming gaming society.

The 1990s saw a vital second in the beginning of esports with the arrival of "Road Warrior II." This exemplary battling game by Capcom reclassified the class as well as presented the idea of cutthroat gaming. "Road Contender II" highlighted no holds barred fights, where players could challenge each other in arcade settings, laying out a cutthroat gaming society that actually flourishes today.

It was during this period that the possibility of expert gamers started to come to fruition. Cutthroat players in games like "Road Contender II" and "Mortal Kombat" acquired acknowledgment and, surprisingly, humble sponsorships for their abilities. Gaming magazines started to cover these players, and provincial and public contests stood out from both gamers and traditional press.

The idea of esports got a critical lift with the arrival of "Shake" in 1996. This first-individual shooter game by id Programming advocated the class as well as presented the idea of online multiplayer gaming. "Tremor" permitted players to contend with each other over the web, separating geological boundaries and preparing for the worldwide esports local area we see today.

In South Korea, one more essential crossroads in the historical backdrop of esports was occurring. The nation, known for serious areas of strength for its way of life and trend setting innovation, was facilitating cutthroat gaming occasions known as "PC bangs." These web bistros gave a space to players to meet up, contend, and exhibit their abilities in games like "StarCraft."

The arrival of "StarCraft" in 1998 denoted a defining moment in the esports scene. The continuous technique game by Snowstorm Diversion turned into a social peculiarity in South Korea. It was a game as well as a public game, with players and groups accomplishing big name status. Telecasters like OGN (Ongamenet) started circulating "StarCraft" competitions, and the games were even displayed on standard TV, acquainting esports with a more extensive crowd.

The serious "StarCraft" scene in South Korea was described by proficient players, group houses, and committed fan followings. Players like Lee "Faker" Sang-hyeok, Lim "NesTea" Jae-Duk, and Jang "MC" Min Chul became easily recognized names, and the contention between top groups like KT Rolster and SK Telecom T1 caught the country's creative mind.

The progress of "StarCraft" in South Korea made a layout for the development of esports in different districts. It showed the way that proficient players, coordinated associations, and organized contest could hoist cutthroat gaming to another level. Esports associations and associations started to arise, making way for the worldwide peculiarity we know today.

The 2000s denoted the start of the esports business as we figure out it now. This period saw the foundation of expert gaming associations, with names like Fnatic and Group Fluid entering the scene. These associations furnished players with monetary help, preparing offices, and assets, making it workable for them to commit themselves to cutthroat gaming full-time.

Esports associations and competitions additionally turned out to be more coordinated. Significant rivalries like the Electronic Games World Cup (ESWC), the World Digital Games (WCG), and the Intel Outrageous Bosses (IEM) acquired conspicuousness, offering significant monetary rewards and worldwide acknowledgment. These competitions drew players from everywhere the world and displayed the global allure of esports.

The progress to web based gaming was a distinct advantage for esports. The ascent of fast web associations, improved netcode, and the rise of stages like Xbox Live and PlayStation Organization empowered players to contend in different games on the web. This shift extended the extent of cutthroat gaming, permitting players to challenge adversaries from various areas of the planet and shaping the reason for the worldwide esports environment.

The ascent of streaming stages, especially Jerk, denoted another huge defining moment in the esports business. Streaming permitted proficient gamers to communicate their ongoing interaction to a worldwide crowd, leading to another age of esports superstars. Watchers could watch their #1 players in real life, gain from their procedures, and even connect with them progressively through talk. This immediate commitment among players and fans was a distinct advantage, as it made a more private and personal association, something that conventional games had attempted to accomplish.

This period additionally saw the ascent of titles that would become staples in the esports world, including "Counter-Strike," "Dota 2," and "Class of Legends." These games pulled in enormous player bases as well as secured themselves as cutthroat titles with flourishing proficient scenes. The association of significant competitions like The Global for "Dota 2" and the Class of Legends Big showdown established the spot of these games at the front of esports.

Notwithstanding players, committed esports pundits and examiners, frequently alluded to as casters, play had a huge impact in the business' prosperity. Casters give in depth discourse, examination, and amusement during esports communicates, assisting watchers with grasping the subtleties of the game and building energy. A large number of them have become as famous as the actual players, forming the story of esports rivalries and making essential minutes.

The ascent of expert players as big names denoted one more defining moment in the esports business. Gamers like Faker in "Class of Legends," s1mple in "Counter-Strike: Worldwide Hostile," and Ninja in "Fortnite" have become commonly recognized names, rising above the gaming scene and showing up in traditional press.

These players, with their uncommon abilities and drawing in characters, have drawn in fans past the gaming local area and brought esports into the standard.

Notwithstanding players, devoted esports reporters and examiners, frequently alluded to as casters, play had a huge impact in the business' prosperity. Casters give in depth critique, examination, and diversion during esports communicates, assisting watchers with grasping the subtleties of the game and building energy. Large numbers of them have become as notorious as the actual players, molding the account of esports contests and making critical minutes.

As esports kept on advancing, the business started to embrace components from conventional games. Diversifying, demonstrated after pro athletics associations like the NBA and NFL, was presented in associations, for example, the Overwatch Association and the Class of Legends Title Series (LCS). Diversifying carried monetary soundness to esports by permitting group proprietors to put resources into a drawn out future with a dependable spot in the association. It pulled in conventional games associations like the New York Yankees and the Dallas Cattle rustlers, who saw the capability of esports and put vigorously in it.

Organized associations and normalized governs additionally added impressive skill to esports. Rather than an assortment of dispersed competitions, many games currently have laid out associations with ordinary seasons and end of the season games. This configuration not just given a more solid timetable to fans yet additionally pulled in customary games associations.

One more fundamental part of the esports example of overcoming adversity is the energetic and connected with local area of fans. Their commitment, backing, and excitement play had a huge impact in the business' development. Fans have filled fields and arenas for esports occasions, and millions more have watched on the web. The energetic fan base has gotten .

1.1 The early days of competitive gaming

The beginning of serious gaming are an intriguing excursion into the starting points of esports, a world that presently flaunts proficient players, multimillion-dollar competitions, and a huge number of committed fans. These early days were while gaming was still in its earliest stages, and the idea of expert serious gaming was at this point to come to fruition completely. To genuinely comprehend the foundations of esports, we should turn back the clock to a time when computer games were simply starting to spellbind the world.

The earliest type of cutthroat gaming can be followed back to the introduction of computer games themselves, which arose during the mid-twentieth 100 years. Everything began with "Tennis for Two," a fundamental tennis reenactment game made in 1958 by physicist William Higinbotham on an oscilloscope show. While this game might appear to be crude by the present guidelines, it was a historic move toward the development of computerized diversion and laid the foundation for video gaming.

The resulting many years saw the arrival of a few famous games that formed the gaming scene, including "Pong" in 1972 and "Space Trespassers" in 1978. These games, albeit basic by contemporary principles, caught the creative mind of players and laid out the establishment for what might ultimately become cutthroat gaming.

The rise of arcades was a vital improvement during the beginning of gaming. These foundations permitted individuals to accumulate and play computer games in a group environment. Arcades denoted the introduction of collective gaming encounters and acquainted players with the idea of going up against each other in different titles.

During the 1980s, the serious gaming scene started to come to fruition. The arrival of "Room Trespassers" had previously made way for serious gaming, yet it was the "Brilliant Period of Arcades" that carried this idea to the front. Players ran to arcades to challenge each other in games like "Pac-Man," "Jackass Kong," and "Road Warrior."

While these early contests were casual and frequently founded on high scores or one-on-one fights, they established the groundwork for the eventual fate of serious gaming. Players started to perceive and value the ability expected to succeed in these games, and some would proceed to turn into the original serious gamers.

The 1980s likewise saw the ascent of the first perceived esports occasion — the "Space Trespassers Title" coordinated by Atari in 1980. This opposition was a huge achievement as it pulled in north of 10,000 members from around the US. While the awards were humble by the present principles, with the primary spot victor getting a regular arcade game, the occasion showed the developing interest in serious gaming.

Regardless of the early acknowledgment and energy for cutthroat gaming, the business was still in its outset, coming up short on the foundation and backing expected to form into the worldwide peculiarity we know today.

The arrival of home gaming consoles like the Atari 2600 and the Nintendo Theater setup (NES) during the 1980s denoted a urgent crossroads throughout the entire existence of computer games. These control center brought the gaming experience into the lounge rooms of millions of families. Interestingly, players could partake in the excitement of computer games from the solace of their own homes.

The openness of home gaming consoles assisted cultivate a developing gaming with refined. It wasn't just about visiting arcades any longer; families and people could now appreciate computer games out of the blue. This change in the manner games were played would become instrumental in the development of serious gaming.

The 1990s were a groundbreaking time for cutthroat gaming. It was during this decade that the idea of expert gamers started to come to fruition. The arrival of "Road Warrior II" by Capcom in 1991 denoted a critical defining moment in serious gaming. This famous battling game reclassified the class as well as presented the idea of cutthroat gaming to a more extensive crowd.

"Road Warrior II" highlighted no holds barred fights, where players could challenge each other in arcade settings. This configuration permitted players to show their abilities, system, and execution. It was these player-versus-player communications that established the groundwork for cutthroat gaming as far as we might be concerned today.

With "Road Warrior II," players could demonstrate their strength over others, and the game immediately turned into a social movement. Serious players would meet in arcades, testing each other to extraordinary fights. The idea of nearby competitions started to come to fruition, as players coordinated occasions to test their abilities and guarantee gloating freedoms.

This cutthroat soul stretched out to other battling games, for example, "Mortal Kombat" and "Tekken," which further advocated the class. Players could now contend in one-on-one fights, exhibiting their dominance of unpredictable combos and character procedures. While the prizes were much of the time little — like free credits at the arcade — the feeling of rivalry was sufficient to drive players to succeed in these games.

During this period, gaming magazines and distributions started to cover serious players, carrying acknowledgment to their abilities and accomplishments. These magazines highlighted player profiles, methodology guides, and competition inclusion. While the awards stayed unobtrusive, the development of a serious gaming society was obvious.

During the 1990s, the appearance of home gaming consoles additionally worked with cutthroat gaming. Games like "Crush Brothers." on the Nintendo 64 and "Can-do attitude" on the Super Nintendo furnished players with the valuable chance to challenge their companions in the solace of their own homes. These titles carried serious gaming to a more open and broad crowd, laying the basis for the future development of esports.

During this time, the idea of esports was still in its early stages, and the foundation for proficient cutthroat gaming was generally nonexistent. There were no coordinated associations, proficient players, or huge monetary prizes. Cutthroat gaming stayed a grassroots development, driven by enthusiastic players who tried to demonstrate their abilities and achieve acknowledgment.

It was in the last part of the 1990s and mid 2000s that cutthroat gaming saw a critical jump forward with the arrival of "Tremor" in 1996. This first-individual shooter game by id Programming promoted the class as well as presented the idea of online multiplayer gaming to a more extensive crowd.

"Tremor" permitted players to go up against one another over the web, separating geological obstructions and making ready for the worldwide esports local area we see today. The capacity to challenge rivals from various regions of the planet was a distinct advantage, making it workable for players to demonstrate their abilities on a worldwide scale.

"Tremor" competitions and contests started to arise, drawing in players from around the world. While the awards were still moderately little, the acknowledgment and feeling of local area were significant. Serious gaming was not generally restricted to nearby arcades or social occasions; it had turned into a worldwide peculiarity.

The cutthroat "Shudder" scene laid the preparation for proficient players and the early esports associations that would follow. While the business was still distant from the multimillion-dollar competitions and enormous scope associations we see today, the seeds of expert cutthroat gaming had been planted.

The turn of the thousand years was a significant period for the improvement of esports. Cutthroat gaming was developing, and the framework was starting to come to fruition. Associations and associations started to arise, giving players valuable chances to contend and acquire acknowledgment.

In South Korea, a country with a solid gaming society and trend setting innovation framework, the serious gaming scene was taking off. Web bistros, known as "PC bangs," gave a space to players to meet up, contend, and grandstand their abilities in games like "StarCraft."

The arrival of "StarCraft" in 1998 denoted a defining moment in the historical backdrop of esports. The ongoing technique game by Snowstorm Diversion turned into a social peculiarity in South Korea. It was a game as well as a public game, with players and groups accomplishing big name status. Telecasters like OGN (Ongamenet) started broadcasting "StarCraft" competitions, and the games were even displayed on standard TV, acquainting esports with a more extensive crowd.

In South Korea, the cutthroat "StarCraft" scene was described by proficient players, group houses, and devoted fan followings. Players like Lee "Faker" Sang-hyeok, Lim "NesTea" Jae-Duk, and Jang "MC" Min Chul became commonly recognized names, and the contention between top groups like KT Rolster and SK Telecom T1 caught the country's creative mind.

The progress of "StarCraft" in South Korea made a layout for the development of esports in different districts. It showed the way that proficient players, coordinated associations, and organized rivalry could raise cutthroat gaming to another level. Esports associations and associations started to arise, making way for the worldwide peculiarity we know today.

During a similar period, in the Western world, cutthroat gaming was building up some forward momentum. Significant rivalries like the Electronic Games World Cup (ESWC), the World Digital Games (WCG), and the Intel Outrageous Experts (IEM) acquired conspicuousness, offering significant monetary rewards and worldwide acknowledgment. These competitions pulled in players from everywhere the world, displaying the global allure of esports.

The progress to web based gaming was a distinct advantage for esports. The ascent of rapid web associations, improved netcode, and the rise of stages like Xbox Live and PlayStation Organization empowered players to contend in different games on the web. This shift extended the extent of serious gaming, permitting players to challenge adversaries from various regions of the planet and framing the reason for the worldwide esports biological system.

1.2 Pioneers who laid the foundation

The example of overcoming adversity of esports, as far as we might be concerned today, was made conceivable by the spearheading people and gatherings who established the groundwork for the business. These visionaries, driven by their enthusiasm for gaming, cutthroat soul, and an unflinching faith in the capability of esports, assumed critical parts in molding the scene of expert serious gaming. Their commitment, advancement, and readiness to rock the boat have made a permanent imprint on the business.

One of the earliest trailblazers of cutthroat gaming was Walter Day, a name inseparable from the exemplary arcade gaming time. Walter Day, a secondary teacher from Iowa, is frequently credited with beginning the cutthroat gaming development. In 1982, he established Twin Systems, an association that tracked high scores in arcade games. Twin Universes filled in as the authority scorekeeper for computer game records and turned into a focal center point for cutthroat gamers.

Day's vision was to perceive and praise the accomplishments of gamers who accomplished high scores in exemplary arcade games like "Jackass Kong," "Pac-Man," and "Space rocks." He coordinated the very first "Twin Cosmic systems Public Computer game Group" in 1983, perceiving top players and offering them an open door to exhibit their abilities. This move laid the preparation for cutthroat gaming by legitimizing the possibility of expert gamers.

The endeavors of Walter Day and Twin Universes were instrumental in hoisting the situation with cutthroat gamers. They helped shift the impression of gaming from an easygoing distraction to a real cutthroat pursuit. The documentation of high scores and the acknowledgment of top players carried a feeling of authenticity to the universe of cutthroat gaming, making way for future improvements in the business.

In the domain of battling games, Tomo Ohira, known as the "The Legend" in the cutthroat "Road Warrior II" people group, was a spearheading figure. Ohira was a prevailing player in the beginning of serious "Road Warrior II" competitions in Southern California. He was famous for his uncommon abilities with Ryu and Ken, two of the game's notorious characters.

Tomo Ohira's impact stretched out past his gaming ability. He was instrumental in sorting out and advancing nearby "Road Contender II" competitions in Southern California, uniting players to contend and share their adoration for the game. These early competitions filled in as a forerunner to the coordinated esports occasions we see today.

Tomo Ohira's commitment to "Road Warrior II" promoted the game as a serious title and established the groundwork for the "Road Contender" establishment's heritage in cutthroat gaming. His commitments, both as a player and a local area coordinator, assumed a critical part in molding the battling game scene.

One more outstanding trailblazer in the realm of cutthroat gaming is Billy Mitchell, a name notable in the arcade gaming local area. Mitchell accomplished distinction for his extraordinary abilities in exemplary games like "Jackass Kong" and "Pac-Man." He was among the main players to accomplish an ideal score in "Pac-Man," procuring him a spot in gaming history.

Billy Mitchell's serious soul and record-breaking accomplishments caught the consideration of gamers and the media. His quest for high scores and the acknowledgment of his accomplishments by associations like Twin Cosmic systems raised the situation with serious gaming. Mitchell's commitments featured the ability and devotion expected to succeed in arcade gaming and established the groundwork for cutthroat gaming's development.

During a similar period, proficient gaming groups started to shape, denoting a critical stage in the development of esports. One of the earliest and most famous gaming groups was "The Brilliant Period of Gaming" (Posse), established by Dennis Fong, otherwise called "Sift." Sift was a trailblazer in the first-individual shooter kind, earning respect for his abilities in games like "Destruction" and "Shudder."

Sift's accomplishments in aggressive gaming were exploring. He turned into the world's most memorable expert gamer when he won John Carmack's Ferrari 328 GTS as the stupendous award at the Red Obliteration "Shake" competition in 1997. This obvious a defining moment in cutthroat gaming, as it exhibited the potential for proficient players to procure significant prizes and acknowledgment.

Sift's making of Group, one of the earliest gaming groups, exhibited the rise of expert esports associations. Group comprised of top players in different games, and the group effectively took part in competitions and shows. This model of coordinated gaming groups set up for the development of esports associations later on.

The ascent of esports associations like Fnatic and Group Fluid could never have been conceivable without the spearheading endeavors of Sift and Posse. These early groups carried construction and incredible skill to serious gaming, giving players monetary help, preparing offices, and assets to devote themselves to their specialty.

The development of cutthroat gaming likewise saw the rise of esports reporters and experts, frequently alluded to as "casters." These people assumed a critical part in molding the story of esports contests and making significant minutes for fans. One of the trailblazers in this field is James "2GD" Harding.

James "2GD" Harding, a previous expert gamer himself, progressed into a profession as an esports caster and host. His particular style, mind, and profound comprehension of the games he covered made him a dearest figure in the esports local area. As a caster, he gave in depth editorial, examination, and diversion during esports communicates.

2GD's commitments to the universe of projecting aided make esports more available and connecting with for watchers. He brought a degree of diversion and knowledge that upgraded the review insight, making esports occasions more charming and open to a more extensive crowd.

While these spearheading people and gatherings assumed vital parts in molding the early scene of cutthroat gaming, there were other powerful figures who added to the business' development. In any case, the advancement of esports wasn't restricted to explicit people; it was an aggregate exertion that elaborate energetic players, coordinators, and networks meeting up to understand the capability of cutthroat gaming.

The beginning of serious gaming were described by a feeling of investigation and trial and error. The trailblazers of the business didn't have a clear cut way to follow, and they confronted different difficulties and obstructions en route. However, their commitment, development, and faith in the groundbreaking force of gaming prepared for the advanced esports environment.

As the esports business kept on developing, it entered another time characterized by the foundation of organized associations and normalized guidelines. These improvements added impressive skill and solidness to the business, making it more interesting to financial backers, supports, and a more extensive crowd.

The ascent of streaming stages, especially Jerk, denoted another huge defining moment in the esports business. Streaming permitted proficient gamers to communicate their ongoing interaction to a worldwide crowd, leading to another age of esports superstars. Watchers could watch their number one players in real life, gain from their systems, and even collaborate with them continuously through talk. This immediate commitment among players and fans was a distinct advantage, as it made a more private and close association, something that customary games had attempted to accomplish.

The idea of esports got a critical lift with the arrival of "StarCraft" in 1998. This continuous procedure game by Snowstorm Diversion turned into a social peculiarity in South Korea. It was a game as well as a public game, with players and groups accomplishing big name status. Telecasters like OGN (Ongamenet) started broadcasting "StarCraft" competitions, and the games were even displayed on standard TV, acquainting esports with a more extensive crowd.

1.3 Evolution of gaming tournaments

The development of gaming competitions is a dazzling excursion that matches the ascent of cutthroat gaming, or esports, itself. From humble starting points in arcades and little social occasions, gaming competitions have changed into enormous scope, around the world perceived occasions, drawing a large number of members and watchers. This change has been driven by a mix of innovative progressions, expanded openness, developing interest, and the commitment of players, coordinators, and patrons.

The beginning of gaming competitions were set apart by casual, local area driven occasions, frequently held in arcades or other social spaces where computer games were accessible. These social occasions gave an open door to players to grandstand their abilities, challenge their companions, and, now and again, go after humble awards. Players would accumulate around arcade cupboards, home control center, or PCs, taking part in agreeable competition and brotherhood.

One of the main recorded gaming competitions was the "Space Trespassers Title" coordinated by Atari in 1980. This occasion, held at different areas across the US, pulled in more than 10,000 members. While the opposition was moderately basic and zeroed in on accomplishing high scores, it exhibited the developing interest in serious gaming and established the groundwork for future gaming competitions.

Arcades assumed a crucial part in the early gaming competition scene. These social spaces gave a focal center point to gamers to gather and contend. Players would take part in challenges to see who could accomplish the most noteworthy scores or complete games with the least missteps. These challenges were the forerunners to present day gaming competitions, where players would ultimately contend in different titles, sorts, and organizations.

During the 1980s, the serious gaming scene started to come to fruition with the arrival of well known arcade games like "Pac-Man," "Jackass Kong," and "Road Warrior." These games offered cutthroat components, for example, high-score difficulties and straight on fights, which reverberated with players trying to demonstrate their gaming ability.

The development of battling games like "Road Warrior II" in 1991 significantly affected gaming competitions. This famous title presented the idea of player-versus-player rivalry, making way for coordinated cutthroat gaming. Players assembled in arcades, bars, and different settings to challenge one another, frequently partaking in single-end sections or cooperative rivalries.

These early battling game competitions were casual yet exceptionally cutthroat. They pulled in committed players and started to draw the consideration of gaming magazines and distributions. These distributions highlighted player profiles, methodology guides, and inclusion of competition results, further legitimizing the cutthroat gaming scene.

During this period, the idea of esports was still in its early stages, and the framework for proficient serious gaming was generally nonexistent. While the serious gaming scene was unstructured and rewards were in many cases unassuming, the feeling of rivalry and brotherhood was sufficient to fuel the energy of players.

The progress to home gaming consoles during the 1980s and 1990s extended the compass of gaming competitions. Games like "Crush Brothers." on the Nintendo 64 and "Mental fortitude" on the Super Nintendo permitted players to challenge their companions in the solace of their own homes. These titles carried cutthroat gaming to a more open and far reaching crowd, laying the basis for the future development of esports.

The development of web based gaming denoted a critical achievement in the advancement of gaming competitions. Online multiplayer capacities, improved netcode, and the approach of stages like Xbox Live and PlayStation Organization permitted players to contend in different games over the web. This shift extended the extent of cutthroat gaming, making it workable for players to challenge adversaries from various regions of the planet and structure the reason for the worldwide esports environment.

The last part of the 1990s and mid 2000s denoted a urgent period for the improvement of esports. Serious gaming was building up some decent forward momentum, and the foundation was starting to come to fruition. Associations and associations started to arise, giving players potential chances to contend and acquire acknowledgment.

In South Korea, a country with a solid gaming society and trend setting innovation framework, the cutthroat gaming scene was taking off. Web bistros, known as "PC bangs," gave a space to players to meet up, contend, and grandstand their abilities in games like "StarCraft."

The arrival of "StarCraft" in 1998 was a defining moment in the historical backdrop of esports. This constant system game by Snowstorm Diversion turned into a social peculiarity in South Korea. It was a game as well as a public game, with players and groups accomplishing big name status. Telecasters like OGN (Ongamenet) started circulating "StarCraft" competitions, and the games were even displayed on standard TV, acquainting esports with a more extensive crowd.

In South Korea, the cutthroat "StarCraft" scene was portrayed by proficient players, group houses, and committed fan followings. Players like Lee "Faker" Sang-hyeok, Lim "NesTea" Jae-Duk, and Jang "MC" Min Chul became commonly recognized names, and the competition between top groups like KT Rolster and SK Telecom T1 caught the country's creative mind.

The outcome of "StarCraft" in South Korea made a layout for the development of esports in different districts. It showed the way that proficient players, coordinated associations, and organized contest could lift serious gaming to another level. Esports associations and associations started to arise, making way for the worldwide peculiarity we know today.

During a similar period, in the Western world, cutthroat gaming was building up some decent momentum. Significant contests like the Electronic Games World Cup (ESWC), the World Digital Games (WCG), and the Intel Outrageous Bosses (IEM) acquired conspicuousness, offering significant monetary rewards and worldwide acknowledgment. These competitions pulled in players from everywhere the world, displaying the global allure of esports.

The last part of the 1990s and mid 2000s denoted the start of the esports business as we grasp it now. This period saw the foundation of expert gaming associations, with names like Fnatic and Group Fluid entering the scene. These associations furnished players with monetary help, preparing offices, and assets, making it feasible for them to devote themselves to serious gaming full-time.

Esports associations and competitions additionally turned out to be more coordinated. Significant rivalries like the Electronic Games World Cup (ESWC), the

World Digital Games (WCG), and the Intel Outrageous Experts (IEM) acquired conspicuousness, offering significant monetary rewards and worldwide acknowledgment. These competitions drew players from everywhere the world and exhibited the global allure of esports.

The ascent of expert esports associations like Fnatic and Group Fluid denoted a critical change in the serious gaming scene. These associations carried design and incredible skill to cutthroat gaming, furnishing players with monetary help, preparing offices, and assets to commit themselves to their specialty. As these associations developed, they ventured into different game titles, framing esports groups that contended in different sorts and organizations.

The mid 2000s were a time of trial and error and development for esports. The foundation of significant contests and the development of expert associations started to lay the basis for a practical esports environment. These improvements permitted players to seek after esports as a full-time vocation, procure huge rewards, and earn respect as expert gamers.

The quick development of the web and the accessibility of rapid associations made ready for another time in esports. Internet web based stages, especially Jerk, reformed the way esports occasions were communicated and consumed. These stages permitted proficient gamers to communicate their ongoing interaction to a worldwide crowd, empowering fans to watch their #1 players in real life and cooperate with them progressively.

Jerk, sent off in 2011, immediately turned into the main stage for esports streaming. It offered an easy to understand interface that permitted players to share their gaming encounters, give critique, and draw in with their crowds. Watchers could observe live transmissions, buy into their number one decorations, and collaborate through talk. This degree of direct commitment among players and fans was uncommon in the realm of sports and amusement.

The development of streaming stages raised esports higher than ever. It not just given a stage to proficient gamers to grandstand their abilities and characters yet in addition permitted fans to turn out to be essential for the gaming experience. The intuitive idea of streaming, with ongoing visit and crowd cooperation, made areas of strength for an of local area and network.

Streaming stages likewise assumed a basic part in the improvement of esports famous people. Proficient gamers, decorations, and content makers acquired enormous followings and secured themselves as compelling figures in the gaming local area. Decorations like Tyler "Ninja" Blevins, Michael "Cover" Grzesiek, and Imane "Pokimane" Anys became commonly recognized names, hoarding a huge number of supporters and producing significant pay through their streams.

The availability and worldwide reach of streaming stages additionally energized the development of gaming competitions. Esports occasions, whether they were significant global titles or more modest local area competitions, could now be watched by a huge number of watchers from everywhere the world. This perceivability pulled in patrons, publicists, and financial backers, offering monetary help for the two players and coordinators.

Chapter 2

Professional Players - The Heart of the Game

Proficient players are obviously the core of the esports business. These people, who commit their lives to culminating their specialty, address the most significant level of ability and rivalry in the realm of cutthroat gaming. As the essence of esports, they rouse and dazzle crowds with their unimaginable ability, devotion, and enthusiasm for their picked games. This segment investigates the significant job that proficient players play in the development and outcome of esports.

The way to turning into an expert esports player isn't not normal for that of conventional competitors. It requires a blend of ability, difficult work, responsibility, and a profound comprehension of the game. These players put innumerable hours into leveling up their abilities, dominating game mechanics, and creating procedures to beat their rivals. Much of the time, they start their excursion very early on, attracted to the appeal of cutthroat gaming and the fantasy about arriving at the zenith of their picked discipline.

Proficient players come from different foundations and societies, mirroring the worldwide allure of esports. They can be tracked down in each side of the world, contending in a great many game types, from first-individual shooters and ongoing methodology games to sports reproductions and collectible games. The variety of esports guarantees that players with different interests and ranges of abilities can track down their specialty inside the business.

One of the main traits of expert players is their steady hard working attitude. They contribute an exceptional measure of time and exertion into their art, with training meetings that can reach out for a long time every day. Esports expects players to continually refine their abilities, adjust to evolving metagames (the present status of the game's equilibrium and procedure), and remain in front of the opposition. This degree of commitment is much the same as the preparation regimens of conventional competitors, mirroring the professionalization of serious gaming.

Proficient players are continually pushing the limits of what is conceivable inside a game. They are not satisfied with simply arriving at a high expertise level; they plan to rethink the restrictions of human execution inside their separate titles. This desire has prompted the making of stunning minutes and showcases of expertise that enthrall crowds and have enduring effects.

As well as dominating the mechanics of their games, proficient players should likewise develop their psychological backbone. Esports can intellectually burden, with extreme contest, high stakes, and the steady strain to perform at a reliably significant level. Players should foster versatility, center, and close to home control to endure the requests of expert play. Emotional well-being and prosperity have become progressively significant subjects in esports, with associations and associations executing emotionally supportive networks to assist players with adapting to the difficulties they face.

The commitment and diligence of expert players reach out past individual ability advancement. They frequently join esports associations and groups, where they capability as the two contenders and delegates. These associations give players the assets and backing they need to zero in on their presentation. Esports groups offer preparation offices, training staff, investigators, and admittance to top-level gear. The collaboration among players and associations is essential for progress in the business.

Proficient players additionally have the valuable chance to construct their own brands. A considerable lot of them become compelling figures in the gaming local area, hoarding enormous followings via online entertainment and streaming stages. Through live transfers, YouTube channels, and drawing in satisfied, they associate with fans, share their encounters, and give knowledge into the universe of expert gaming. These players are something beyond contenders; they are diplomats for the esports business.

Esports players habitually partake in competitions and associations, displaying their abilities on a worldwide stage. These occasions range from neighborhood rivalries to global titles, offering huge monetary rewards and the opportunity to procure notoriety and acknowledgment. Significant competitions, for example, The Global for "Dota 2" and the Class of Legends Big showdown, are watched by a great many watchers and deal extravagant award pools. These competitions furnish proficient players with the chance to show off their abilities as the best on the planet and secure their place in esports history.

The cutthroat soul of expert players is a main impetus in esports. They blossom with the tension of high-stakes matches and the excitement of rivalry. They comprehend that esports isn't simply a distraction however a requesting vocation that requires consistent improvement and transformation. Proficient players embrace the test and lift the degree of contest, pushing each other higher than ever.

Notwithstanding individual accomplishments, proficient players frequently address their separate nations on the global stage. Esports contests, similar as the

Olympics, highlight public groups going after magnificence. These occasions, like the Overwatch World Cup and the Class of Legends Big showdown, bring players from different nations together to vie for public pride. These global competitions make a special feeling of brotherhood and rivalry, as players wear their nation's tones and endeavor to bring back triumph.

Esports players have particular characters and styles that charm them to fans. Some are known for their extraordinary concentration and determined play, while others are praised for their garish and forceful strategies. The variety of playstyles and characters inside the expert player local area adds profundity and lavishness to the esports experience, as fans can find players who resound with their own inclinations.

The ascent of streaming stages, especially Jerk, significantly affects the connection between proficient players and their fans. Streaming permits players to communicate their ongoing interaction, draw in with watchers through live visit, and make a feeling of closeness that was beforehand unreachable. Fans have the chance to watch their #1 players practice, talk about methodology, and even associate progressively. This immediate collaboration has encouraged areas of strength for an of local area and fan devotion.

Proficient players likewise put resources into their appearance and picture, with a considerable lot of them taking on personas or pen names mirror their gaming characters. These gaming personas frequently become notorious, helping players stick out and interface with their fan base. For instance, Lee "Faker" Sang-hyeok, an unbelievable Class of Legends player, is known for his quiet and unflappable disposition, while Dominique "SonicFox" McLean, a productive battling game player, embraces a fox-themed persona. These characters add to the moxy and allure of expert players.

The esports business has seen the development of hotshots, rising above the limits of cutthroat gaming to become standard superstars. Players like Faker, who has won different Class of Legends Big showdowns, are praised inside the gaming local area as well as in the more extensive mainstream society. These players are welcome to occasions, highlighted in notices, and perceived for their commitments to the business.

Monetary open doors for proficient players have developed essentially, with top players acquiring significant livelihoods from compensations, competition rewards, and sponsorships. Esports associations, driven by speculation and sponsorship bargains, can offer players six-figure pay rates and prize pools that rival those of customary games. These monetary motivations have made proficient gaming a practical and appealing profession way for some.

The peculiarity of esports has turned into a worldwide social power, with proficient players filling in as envoys for the business. They travel to various nations, meet fans from assorted foundations, and experience the overall allure of esports. Players have the special honor of addressing their districts, associations, and themselves on a worldwide scale, encouraging associations that rise above lines and dialects.

While proficient players are commended for their achievements and commitments to esports, they likewise face different difficulties. One of the main difficulties is player burnout. The requesting preparing plans, travel responsibilities, and consistent rivalry can negatively affect players' psychological and actual wellbeing. Player burnout is a huge worry in the business, prompting drives pointed toward advancing player wellbeing and balance between fun and serious activities.

The issue of match-fixing and cheating is one more test that proficient players and the business overall should address. The serious idea of esports, joined with the potential for significant monetary benefits, has prompted cases of match-fixing and conning outrages.

2.1 Profiles of renowned e-sports athletes

Famous esports competitors are the stars of the business, spellbinding crowds with their unbelievable expertise, devotion, and charm. These competitors have ascended to the highest point of their separate games, accomplishing amazing status and gathering gave fan followings. In this segment, we'll investigate profiles of probably the most eminent esports competitors who have made a permanent imprint on the business.

1. **Lee "Faker" Sang-hyeok (Class of Legends)**

   Frequently alluded to as the "Unkillable Devil Ruler," Lee "Faker" Sang-hyeok is seemingly the most popular name in Class of Legends. Hailing from South Korea, Faker has been a prevailing power in the game since the beginning of cutthroat Class of Legends. He is famous for his flawless mechanics, game sense, and the capacity to convey his group to triumph.

   Faker made his most memorable significant progress in 2013 when he brought home the Big showdown with his group, SK Telecom T1. This triumph denoted the start of his famous lifetime and the ascent of South Korea as a force to be reckoned with in Class of Legends. Faker's reliably elevated degree of play and various title wins have made him a notorious figure in the esports world.

   Notwithstanding his noteworthy vocation accomplishments, Faker is known for his quiet and unflappable attitude, even in high-pressure circumstances. He can pursue basic choices without giving it much thought and execute plays that leave fans in stunningness. His heritage in Class of Legends is gotten, and he keeps on being an unmistakable figure in the business.

2. **Jian "Uzi" Zihao (Class of Legends)**

   Jian "Uzi" Zihao, a Chinese expert Class of Legends player, is broadly viewed as one of the most outstanding Promotion conveys in the game's set of experiences. Uzi's forceful and garish playstyle has procured him an army of fans who respect his mechanical ability and grip exhibitions.

Uzi's excursion to popularity started when he joined Illustrious Club in 2012. He immediately became famous with his forceful and exact playstyle. He became known for his uncommon mechanics and unbelievable group battling abilities. Uzi's contention with other Promotion convey players, as Kim "Deft" Hyuk-kyu and Gao "Ning" Zhen-Ning, added show and fervor to the Class of Legends serious scene.

One of the vital turning points of Uzi's vocation was his second place finish at the 2018 Class of Legends Big showdown, where he played for Regal Never Surrender (RNG). His excellent exhibitions all through the competition cemented his status as a legend in the game. While he reported his retirement in 2020 because of wellbeing concerns, Uzi's effect on the esports world remaining parts significant.

3. **Oleksandr "s1mple" Kostyliev (Counter-Strike: Worldwide Hostile)**

   Oleksandr "s1mple" Kostyliev is a Ukrainian expert Counter-Strike: Worldwide Hostile (CS:GO) player famous for his staggering pointing abilities and flexible playstyle. He is many times considered one of the best CS:GO players on the planet.

   S1mple's excursion to fame started when he joined Natus Vincere (Na'Vi), one of the most notable associations in CS:GO. His exhibitions in high-pressure circumstances, grip plays, and wonderful consistency made him a fundamental piece of Na'Vi's prosperity. He has won different MVP grants at major CS:GO competitions, establishing his standing as a top player.

   One of s1mple's profession features was driving Na'Vi to the amazing finals of the 2018 FACEIT Major, where they barely passed up bringing home the title. In spite of the misfortune, s1mple's singular exhibition was out and out phenomenal, cementing his status as one of the most mind-blowing CS:GO players ever.

4. **Danil "Dendi" Ishutin (Dota 2)**

   Danil "Dendi" Ishutin is a Ukrainian expert Dota 2 player celebrated for his charming character and inventive ongoing interaction. He turned into a commonly recognized name in the Dota 2 local area for his excellent abilities and dynamic playstyle.

   Dendi's ascent to popularity can be followed back to his experience with Natus Vincere (Na'Vi), where he was a central member during the early long periods of cutthroat Dota 2. He assumed a pivotal part in Na'Vi's prosperity, including their next in line finish at The Worldwide 2012 and their title triumph at The Global 2011. Dendi's attractive character and engaging streams charmed him to fans around the world.

   While his cutthroat profession saw its highs and lows, Dendi's effect on Dota

2 and esports in general can't be put into words. He stays a darling figure in the gaming local area and an image of the early long stretches of serious Dota 2.

5. **Choi "Plane" Ji Sung (StarCraft II)**

   Choi "Plane" Ji Sung is a South Korean expert StarCraft II player perceived for his remarkable Terran play and cutthroat accomplishments. He arose as one of the main figures in the StarCraft II esports scene during its initial years.

   Plane's excursion to conspicuousness started in the Korean StarCraft II scene, where he showed his strategic splendor and key authority. He earned worldwide respect when he joined the worldwide esports association Group StarTale. His accomplishments incorporate different title succeeds at renowned StarCraft II competitions and occasions.

   Aircraft's prosperity and exceptional interactivity added to the notoriety of StarCraft II as an esport. His dynamic and engaging matches charmed crowds, and he assumed a significant part in the development of serious StarCraft II.

6. **Gonzalo "ZeRo" Barrios (Crush Brothers.)**

   Gonzalo "ZeRo" Barrios is a Chilean expert Crush Brothers. player known for his predominance in the Really Crush Brothers. for Wii U period. He earned respect for his outstanding expertise, insightful way to deal with the game, and his capacity to keep a long dash of competition triumphs.

   ZeRo's cutthroat process started with Crush Brothers. Fight, however he accomplished amazing status during the Really Crush Brothers. for Wii U time. He partook in an extraordinary run of achievement, winning various competitions and laying down a good foundation for himself as the world's best player. His calculated way to deal with character matchups and exact execution put him aside in the cutthroat scene.

   Notwithstanding his accomplishments as a player, ZeRo turned into an unmistakable substance maker, sharing his insight and experiences on Crush Brothers. through recordings and streams. He assumed a crucial part in developing the Really Crush Brothers. serious local area and encouraging a climate of learning and improvement.

7. **Ilya "Lil" Ilyuk (Dota 2)**

   Ilya "Lil" Ilyuk is a Ukrainian expert Dota 2 player known for his charming character and inventive way to deal with the game. He earned respect for his whimsical methodologies and excellent help play.

   Lil's excursion to popularity started when he joined Virtus.pro, an unmistakable esports association with a solid presence in Dota 2. His creative drafting and in-game direction added to Virtus.pro's outcome in the cutthroat scene. One of his profession features was winning The Culmination 7 of every 2017 with Virtus.pro.

   Lil's strange character and unusual playstyle charmed him to fans and made him a darling figure in the Dota 2 local area. His effect on the game reached out past his in-game abilities, as he carried amusement and imagination to the serious scene.

8. **Lee "Streak" Youthful Ho (StarCraft: Brood War and StarCraft II)**
   Lee "Streak" Youthful Ho, a South Korean expert StarCraft player, is broadly viewed as perhaps of the best player in the historical backdrop of both StarCraft: Brood War and StarCraft II. Streak is commended for his uncommon performing multiple tasks capacities, vital reasoning, and mechanical ability.
   Blaze's vocation started in the StarCraft: Brood War time, where he made exceptional progress. He ruled the scene, coming out on top for various titles and turning into the most youthful player to arrive at the StarCraft Proleague. His progress to StarCraft II brought further achievement, as he kept up with his status as one of the world's top players.
   One of Glimmer's most notorious minutes was his title triumph in the IEM Season IX - Big showdown in 2015. His presentation in the last match against Lee "Development" Shin-Hyung displayed his extraordinary expertise and set his standing as a legend in the StarCraft series.
9. **Sasha "Scarlett" Hostyn (StarCraft II)**
   Sasha "Scarlett" Hostyn, a Canadian expert StarCraft II player, is known for her extraordinary Zerg play and her pivotal accomplishments as a female player in the esports world. Scarlett has demonstrated that orientation isn't a boundary to outcome in cutthroat gaming.
   Scarlett's serious excursion started with StarCraft II, where she immediately rose to conspicuousness as one of the top Zerg players. Her remarkable accomplishments remember triumphs at chief competitions and effective runs for global rivalries. Scarlett's diligence, flexibility, and capacity to contend at the most significant level gained her appreciation in the StarCraft II people group.
   Scarlett's effect on esports stretched out past her singular accomplishments. She motivated hopeful female players and demonstrated that orientation variety isn't an obstruction in the business. Her prosperity added to the continuous endeavors to establish a more comprehensive climate for ladies in esports.
10. **Christopher "GeT_RiGhT" Alesund (Counter-Strike: Worldwide Hostile)**

Christopher "GeT_RiGhT" Alesund is a Swedish expert Counter-Strike: Worldwide Hostile (CS:GO) player celebrated for his momentous life span and consistency in the game. He is in many cases viewed as one of the best CS:GO players on the planet.

GeT_RiGhT's excursion to notoriety started in the early long periods of cutthroat CS:GO. He joined Ninjas in Nightgown (NiP), an unbelievable esports association, and assumed a critical part in NiP's memorable 87-0 series of wins. His uncommon game sense, strategic mindfulness, and grasp exhibitions cemented his status as a top player.

2.2 The commitment, training, and sacrifices of professional gamers

The existence of an expert gamer may appear to be charming, with the appeal of titles, sponsorships, and an army of fans. Notwithstanding, in the background, the excursion to the top is set apart by a mind boggling degree of responsibility, thorough preparation, and critical individual penances. Proficient gamers are not simply specialists; they are committed competitors who work vigorously to consummate their abilities, adjust to the always developing scene of their picked games, and keep up with their strategic advantage.

Obligation to Greatness

The responsibility of expert gamers is steady. A considerable lot of them start their excursion early in life, frequently devoting most of their waking hours to rehearsing and working on their interactivity. This degree of commitment requires enthusiasm and an affection for the game that rises above the possibility of easy-going play. These people try to arrive at the zenith of cutthroat gaming and will take the necessary steps to arrive.

Proficient gamers concentrate intensely on improving their abilities, grasping game mechanics, and dominating the subtleties of their picked titles. They train for hours every day, reliably driving themselves to accomplish new degrees of aptitude. The persevering quest for greatness is a central trait of their responsibility.

Notwithstanding individual practice, proficient gamers every now and again take part in group instructional meetings. These meetings center around correspondence, collaboration, and planning for serious matches. Viable collaboration is fundamental in group based games like Class of Legends and Counter-Strike: Worldwide Hostile, where composed plays and navigation are basic to progress.

Thorough Preparation Regimens

The preparation routine of an expert gamer mirrors that of conventional competitors. The cutthroat gaming scene is profoundly requesting, expecting players to keep up with max execution, both intellectually and genuinely. Preparing plans are thorough, with day to day practice meetings, audit of ongoing interaction film, and examination of in-game systems.

By and large, proficient gamers have devoted mentors and experts who help with their preparation. Mentors give important bits of knowledge into interactivity, technique, and independent direction, assisting players with refining their abilities and become more powerful contenders. These mentors frequently have insight in the game and a profound comprehension of its mechanics.

The psychological part of preparing is similarly as basic as the physical. Proficient gamers center around working on their focus, response time, and dynamic under tension. They take part in activities and exercises that improve their mental capacities and keep a sharp mental edge.

Actual wellbeing is one more feature of preparing that proficient gamers focus on. Keeping a sound way of life through legitimate sustenance, normal activity, and adequate rest is pivotal for maximized operation. Actual prosperity upholds smartness and perseverance during long gaming meetings and competitions.

Transformation and Advancement

Proficient gamers should be versatile and inventive. The universe of esports is dynamic, with game designers regularly delivering updates and equilibrium changes that can altogether influence ongoing interaction. Players should keep awake to date with these progressions and immediately adjust their techniques and strategies to stay cutthroat.

Development is additionally key to remaining ahead in the esports world. Players frequently look for new and whimsical ways to deal with the game, whether it's through remarkable person decisions, methodologies, or strategies. This imaginative soul can prompt weighty plays and methodologies that give them an edge over their adversaries.

Keeping a harmony among consistency and development is a fine art in itself. While consistency in execution is essential, the capacity to amaze adversaries with new methodologies keeps the serious scene energizing and dynamic. This versatility and advancement are characteristics that characterize proficient gamers and put them aside from relaxed players.

Penances in Quest for Greatness

The existence of an expert gamer requires huge individual penances. The requesting preparing plan and the quest for greatness frequently mean forfeiting time with loved ones. Proficient gamers are every now and again separated, going through incalculable hours rehearsing and getting ready for competitions.

Numerous expert gamers likewise forego customary schooling or business chances to seek after their vocations in serious gaming. The choice to zero in on esports as a full-time occupation is a critical a disregard for one's own needs, as it conveys dangers and vulnerabilities. Be that as it may, these people are driven by their enthusiasm for gaming and the longing to succeed in their picked field.

The monetary parts of expert gaming can challenge also. While top players acquire significant wages through compensations, competition rewards, and sponsorships, many hopeful gamers face monetary vulnerability. They might battle to earn enough to pay the bills while seeking after their fantasies in the cutthroat gaming scene. The monetary penances are important for the excursion for the people who try to arrive at the top.

Keeping a solid balance between fun and serious activities can be hard for proficient gamers. The requesting preparing plans, consistent travel, and strain to perform can negatively affect their psychological and actual wellbeing. Burnout is a persevering concern, and players should effectively attempt to offset their esports vocations with individual prosperity.

Pursuing the Fantasy

The responsibility, preparing, and forfeits of expert gamers are driven by the fantasy about turning into the best in their picked games. This fantasy is a strong inspiration that keeps them not entirely set in stone, even despite misfortune. Accomplishing the situation with an expert gamer, with acknowledgment, notoriety, and achievement, is the zenith of their endeavors and a demonstration of their enduring responsibility.

Esports proceeds to develop and advance, with expanding potential open doors and acknowledgment. The responsibility and penances of expert gamers play had a critical impact in forming the business. As the esports environment grows, with bigger award pools, more conspicuous sponsorships, and global acknowledgment, the way to proficient gaming turns out to be really engaging and achievable.

Nonetheless, the excursion stays testing and requires a degree of commitment and assurance that couple of can grasp. The obligation to greatness, thorough preparation regimens, versatility, development, and individual penances characterize the existence of an expert gamer. Their accounts act as a motivation to the people who share the fantasy about accomplishing significance in the realm of serious gaming.

2.3 The rise of e-sports celebrities

The ascent of esports famous people has been an exceptional and groundbreaking peculiarity inside the universe of cutthroat gaming. As the esports business has developed, so too have the characters who address it. These people, frequently proficient players, content makers, or decorations, have risen above the limits of customary gaming networks to accomplish far reaching acknowledgment and popularity. In this part, we'll investigate the elements behind the rise of esports big names and the effect they've had on the business.

1. **Streaming Stages: The Introduction of Individual Brands**

   One of the vital drivers behind the ascent of esports superstars is the coming of streaming stages, especially Jerk. Streaming has upset how crowds associate with and consume gaming content. It has permitted gamers to share their interactivity encounters, characters, and lives with a worldwide crowd continuously.

   Proficient players and content makers the same influence streaming stages to construct their own brands. They utilize their extraordinary characters and abilities to draw in with watchers, cultivating a feeling of local area and association. This degree of direct commitment was uncommon in the realm of sports and diversion, making a more personal connection among fans and their #1 gamers.

   Watchers are attracted to decorations for their interactivity as well as for their critique, humor, and collaboration with the crowd. The legitimacy of streaming substance has led to engaging and congenial gaming characters. This, thus, has made the way to turning into an esports big name more open, as people can exhibit their gifts and construct a following without the requirement for conventional media or huge scope creation.

Streaming stages have democratized acclaim inside the esports business. While proficient players were once the essential figures of the local area, decorations and content makers have cut out their own specialties, considering a more different scope of gaming characters to arise as famous people. This enhancement has improved the business, drawing in various socioeconomics and tastes.

2. **Esports and Diversion Union**

   Esports superstars have added to the union of serious gaming and diversion. They have risen above the gaming scene, showing up in traditional press, teaming up with big names from different businesses, and, surprisingly, seeking after vocations in amusement past gaming. The lines among esports and conventional amusement have obscured, and this union has pushed the acclaim of gaming characters.

   In such manner, esports VIPs have become powerful figures for gamers as well as for the people who have never played a computer game. The capacity to contact a more extensive crowd has fundamentally added to their ascent. Famous people like Tyler "Ninja" Blevins and Michael "Cover" Grzesiek have been highlighted in TV programs, music recordings, and ads, extending their arrive at a long ways past the gaming local area.

   Esports occasions have additionally become additional engaging scenes, with opening functions, live melodic exhibitions, and superstar appearances. This combination of esports and diversion has made a more vivid encounter for crowds and raised the profile of esports famous people.

3. **Individual Marking and Content Creation**

   Individual marking and content creation are fundamental parts of turning into an esports big name. These people make their internet based personas and utilize virtual entertainment, YouTube, and different stages to draw in with fans. Their substance frequently goes past gaming, enveloping video blogs, product, and joint efforts with other powerhouses.

   Esports VIPs perceive the significance of validness and appeal. They frequently share their own lives, encounters, and difficulties with their crowds. This straightforwardness fabricates a more grounded association with fans and encourages a feeling of local area. Watchers frequently follow esports big names for their gaming abilities as well as for their excursion, their battles, and their characters.

   Making connecting with and engaging substance is foremost to developing and keeping a fanbase. Numerous esports superstars are gifted editors, videographers, and web-based entertainment supervisors, it is reliably captivating and great to guarantee that their substance. The capacity to make different and engaging substance is an imperative part of their prosperity.

4. **Fan Commitment and Local area Building**

   Esports famous people focus on fan commitment and local area building. They connect with their fans through live talk, online entertainment, and occasions. Some even include their fans in the innovative flow, permitting them to shape the substance and bearing of their channels.

   Local area building goes past private commitment; it likewise incorporates encouraging a feeling of having a place among fans. Fans frequently relate to a specific esports VIP and interface with similar people locally. Groups of followers, discussions, and Disagreement servers become centers for association and shared energy.

   Fan commitment additionally stretches out to good cause occasions and drives. Numerous esports VIPs utilize their foundation to raise assets for different causes, having a beneficial outcome on society and further charming themselves to their fanbase.

5. **Proficient Contests and Titles**

   Esports superstars as often as possible take part in proficient rivalries and titles. Their exhibitions on these great stages act as a demonstration of their abilities and responsibility, further hardening their status as VIPs inside the business. Significant competitions, like The Global for Dota 2 or the Class of Legends Big showdown, are watched by a great many watchers and proposition significant award pools.

   The serious progress of esports famous people adds to their notoriety and acknowledgment. Bringing home a significant title or accomplishing noteworthy in-game accomplishments lifts their status as unbelievable figures in the esports world. Crowds are enraptured by their interactivity and root for their #1 VIPs as they make progress toward triumph.

6. **Sponsorships and Supports**

   Esports superstars often secure sponsorships and supports from significant brands and organizations. These associations offer monetary help as well as assist with supporting their perceivability and believability. Supports perceive the worth of esports big names in arriving at an educated and drew in crowd.

   Sponsorship arrangements can envelop a scope of chances, from stock coordinated efforts and brand reconciliations in streams to promoting efforts and item supports. These game plans permit esports big names to adapt their notoriety and fabricate their own brands.

7. **Occasions, Shows, and Meet-and-Welcomes**

   Esports superstars frequently show up at occasions, shows, and meet-and-welcomes, where they have the chance to associate with their fans face to face. These occasions give fans an opportunity to meet their #1 characters, get signatures, and take photographs. The actual connection reinforces the connection among VIPs and their fans.

Occasions like gaming shows and exhibitions additionally act as stages for esports famous people to feature their abilities, partake in boards and conversations, and organization with industry experts. These commitment further raise their profile inside the gaming local area.

8. **Rivalry and Contentions**

   Rivalry and contentions are a critical driver of popularity in esports. The extraordinary matches and warmed contentions between players or groups spellbind crowds and add show and energy to the business. Competitions make convincing accounts, and fans frequently energetically support their number one players or groups during these standoffs.

   Prominent competitions, for example, the contention among Faker and Uzi in Class of Legends or the noteworthy matchups between "Ninjas in Night robe" and "Fnatic" in Counter-Strike: Worldwide Hostile, lastingly affect the esports local area. These competitions raise the situation with the elaborate players and groups, attracting fans and driving commitment.

9. **Social and Local Variety**

   The esports world is wealthy in social and local variety. Esports VIPs rise out of various nations and foundations, mirroring the worldwide allure of cutthroat gaming. These people become representatives for their districts, making a feeling of satisfaction and personality inside their networks.

   Social variety and provincial portrayal add to the worldwide idea of esports. Fans from everywhere the world can interface with VIPs who share their social foundation or district. This variety adds profundity to the esports biological system and widens the business' allure.

10. **Challenges and Responsibilites**

While the ascent of esports VIPs has carried various advantages to the business, it has additionally presented difficulties and obligations. The tension of notoriety, the examination of the public eye, and the requests of keeping an individual brand can overpower. Superstars should cautiously deal with their psychological well-being and prosperity, looking for help and equilibrium.

Esports VIPs fundamentally affect their fanbase, and they convey an obligation to capitalize on their leverage for positive change. Many have utilized their foundation to resolve issues like emotional wellness, inclusivity, and variety inside the gaming local area. They advocate for a really inviting and steady climate for gamers, everything being equal.

Chapter 3

Building Winning Teams

Building winning groups in esports is a complicated and diverse undertaking. Serious gaming isn't exclusively a singular pursuit; it depends vigorously on cooperation, coordination, and collaboration among players. Fruitful esports associations and groups perceive the significance of collecting the right blend of ability, sustaining group elements, and cultivating a culture of greatness. This segment dives into the techniques and elements that add to the formation of winning groups in the powerful universe of cutthroat gaming.

Ability Securing: The Groundwork of Progress

The most vital phase in building a triumphant esports group is ability securing. Recognizing and enlisting talented players who supplement the group's targets and playstyle is essential. Groups frequently have exploring and enrollment processes set up to find promising ability.

Proficient players are explored in light of their in-game execution, accomplishments, and similarity with the group's current program. Scouts and administrators survey possible enlisted people's in-game abilities, their capacity to adjust to various systems, and their set of experiences of cooperation and joint effort.

In addition, groups likewise think about the characters and perspectives of imminent players. Fruitful groups search for top-level ability as well as for people who can keep a positive group air and are focused on improving all things considered.

Ability securing isn't restricted to proficient players. Esports associations likewise select mentors, investigators, and care staff who can add to the group's prosperity. Mentors assume a basic part in methodology improvement and player improvement, while experts give significant experiences into rivals' interactivity and assist groups with pursuing information driven choices.

Group Elements and Correspondence

When a group's list is laid out, the following basic step is areas of strength for developing elements and correspondence. In esports, successful correspondence is fundamental, as players should organize their activities continuously to outsmart their adversaries.

Groups frequently cultivate a culture of open and helpful correspondence. Players should feel open to giving input, talking about systems, and resolving issues inside the group. Mentors assume a crucial part in working with this correspondence and assisting players with grasping their jobs and obligations.

Clear and proficient in-game correspondence is pivotal. Players use voice visit or other specialized devices to pass on data about foe developments, technique changes, and strategic choices. This correspondence takes into account fast variations during matches and guarantees that everybody in the group is in total agreement.

Past in-game correspondence, groups likewise center around building trust and fellowship among players. Holding exercises, group building activities, and normal conversations about private and expert improvement add to an amicable group environment.

Vital Preparation and Transformation

Vital arranging is principal to the outcome of an esports group. Groups should foster a profound comprehension of the games they contend in, dissecting in-game mechanics, map systems, character pieces, and metagame patterns. A metagame alludes to the developing systems and character choices that become predominant in a serious climate.

Mentors and examiners work intimately with players to devise methodologies and courses of action. These plans remember subtleties for in-game jobs, strategies, and win conditions. Groups frequently make playbooks, which are assortments of methodologies, to be executed during matches.

Variation is one more basic part of key preparation. Esports games are dynamic, with changes presented through updates, fixes, and equilibrium changes. Groups should be deft and ready to adjust their procedures to stay cutthroat. This flexibility is a vital calculate long haul achievement.

Practice and Preparing Regimens Practice is at the center of a triumphant group's readiness. Groups commit huge opportunity to practice and preparing, expecting to refine their abilities and systems. Preparing regimens frequently incorporate the accompanying components:

Scrimmages: Groups routinely practice against other expert groups by and by matches called scrimmages or scrims. These matches act as a significant recreation of serious play, permitting groups to test their methodologies and coordination.

Individual Expertise Advancement: Players devote time to individual ability improvement. This incorporates sharpening their mechanics, pointing, and in-game capacities. Preparing schedules center around further developing response times and in-game navigation.

Group Activities: Group practices include rehearsing composed plays and techniques. These activities assist players with creating cooperative energy and timing. Mentors and experts assume a huge part in supervising and refining these techniques.

Survey and Investigation: After each training meeting or match, groups audit their ongoing interaction to distinguish regions for development. They watch replays, investigate choices, and examine missteps and triumphs. This post-game investigation is pivotal for learning and development.

Mental Molding: Groups additionally focus on mental molding. Players take part in exercises to keep up with center and smartness during matches. Methods like representation and care assist players with adapting to the strain of rivalry.

Audit of Rivals: In anticipation of serious matches, groups concentrate on their adversaries. They investigate their playstyles, inclinations, and techniques to foster countermeasures and expect their activities.

3.1 The significance of teamwork in e-sports

The meaning of collaboration in esports couldn't possibly be more significant. While individual expertise and ability are fundamental in cutthroat gaming, the aggregate endeavors of a group frequently decide achievement. Esports, as customary games, depend on joint effort, correspondence, and cooperative energy among colleagues to accomplish triumph. In this segment, we will investigate the significant significance of collaboration in esports, its effect on execution, and the systems utilized by proficient groups to encourage powerful cooperation.

1. **The Group Dynamic: Past Individual Expertise**

   In the realm of esports, groups comprise of people with outstanding gaming abilities and ability. These players frequently spend significant time in unambiguous jobs, contingent upon the game they contend in. While individual expertise is positively an essential for proficient gaming, it isn't the sole determinant of progress. What genuinely separates the best groups is their capacity to work as strong units, cooperating to accomplish shared objectives. Group elements stretch out past interactivity. The connections between colleagues, the degree of trust and brotherhood, and the viability of correspondence all assume critical parts in a group's prosperity. Esports groups should work out some kind of harmony between individual greatness and aggregate collaboration.

2. **Viable Correspondence: The Foundation of Collaboration**

   Viable correspondence is the foundation of collaboration in esports. In a speedy and frequently turbulent gaming climate, players should hand-off basic data to their partners quickly. This data can incorporate adversary positions, methodology changes, cooldown status, and strategic choices. Clear and opportune correspondence is fundamental for facilitated interactivity.

   Voice specialized apparatuses like Friction, TeamSpeak, or in-game voice talk are usually utilized by groups to work with ongoing correspondence. Players depend on these instruments to transfer basic data and direction activities, like connecting with the foe, withdrawing, or starting techniques.

Moreover, groups likewise foster a common language or set of callouts to smooth out correspondence. These callouts are speedy, normalized phrases that portray in-game circumstances, permitting players to briefly pass on data. The utilization of callouts limits miscommunication and amplifies the effectiveness of data trade.

3. **Jobs and Obligations: Facilitated Interactivity**

   Esports games are regularly group based, with players taking on unambiguous jobs and obligations. These jobs can differ altogether contingent upon the game. For instance, in a game like Class of Legends, jobs incorporate top laner, jungler, mid laner, Promotion convey, and support. Every job has its one of a kind obligations and goals.

   Facilitated ongoing interaction includes clear job task and understanding. Colleagues should have their very own profound comprehension jobs and the jobs of their partners. This information guarantees that everybody knows their obligations during matches and can really uphold each other.

   The coordination of jobs and obligations reaches out to in-game navigation. Groups foster methodologies and strategies that depend on the novel qualities of every player's job. This cooperative methodology boosts the group's true capacity and takes into consideration a more unique and key ongoing interaction experience.

4. **Collaboration and Group Science**

   Group science and cooperative energy are basic to outcome in esports. These components allude to the immaterial association between colleagues that goes past in-game mechanics. Collaboration empowers players to expect each other's activities, pursue split-subsequent options, and work flawlessly together.

   Accomplishing solid group science takes time and exertion. Groups frequently take part in group building works out, holding exercises, and standard conversations about both individual and expert turn of events. Building trust among colleagues is a vital part of major areas of strength for encouraging.

   The constructive outcomes of collaboration are detectable in the manner groups coordinate their plays. Synergetic groups make dynamic and facilitated plays that frequently shock adversaries. Whether it's executing unpredictable techniques, expertly planned blends of capacities, or elaborate group battles, cooperative energy raises a group's presentation and separates them from less durable rivals.

5. **Versatility and Adaptability**

   In esports, versatility and adaptability are principal to progress. Games are consistently advancing, with designers delivering updates, fixes, and equilibrium changes. Accordingly, techniques that were compelling in the past may presently not be feasible. Groups should stay deft and open to change.

Flexibility reaches out to in-game navigation. Groups need to change their strategies and systems during matches in view of their rival's activities and the steadily changing game state. A readiness to change methodologies on the fly and adjust to startling circumstances is a characteristic of a top-level group.

Furthermore, adaptability likewise connects with the readiness to explore different avenues regarding new techniques and approaches. The best groups constantly advance and push the limits of what is conceivable in the game. Being available to whimsical thoughts can prompt unforeseen victories.

6. **Group The executives and Training**

   Proficient esports groups frequently have committed mentors and care staff to help with group the executives and player improvement. Mentors assume a fundamental part in directing groups, refining their systems, and keeping up with successful group elements. They assist players with grasping their jobs and obligations, recognize regions for development, and work on their in-game direction.

   Mentors additionally work with the audit of interactivity film and post-match examination, where groups take apart their presentation and recognize regions for development. The examination gives important bits of knowledge and assists players with developing collectively.

   Group directors handle the strategic parts of a group's tasks, like planning, travel plans, contract dealings, and liaising with competition coordinators. These help jobs guarantee that players can zero in on their ongoing interaction and planning without the weight of regulatory undertakings.

7. **Arrangement and Practice**

   Readiness and practice are central to making cooperation and progress in esports. Groups commit critical opportunity to rehearse meetings, which incorporate different components:

   Scrimmages: Groups habitually practice against other expert groups practically speaking matches called scrims. These matches give an important recreation of serious play and permit groups to test their techniques and coordination.

   Individual Expertise Advancement: Players concentrate profoundly on leveling up their singular abilities, including mechanics, pointing, and in-game capacities. Preparing schedules intend to further develop response times and independent direction.

   Group Activities: Group practices include rehearsing composed plays and techniques. These activities assist players with creating collaboration and timing. Mentors and experts assume essential parts in managing and refining these systems.

Survey and Investigation: After each training meeting or match, groups audit their interactivity to distinguish regions for development. They watch replays, investigate choices, and talk about slip-ups and triumphs. This post-game investigation is significant for learning and development.

Mental Molding: Mental molding is one more part of readiness. Groups utilize strategies like representation and care to assist players with adapting to the tension of contest, keep up with concentration, and settle on successful in-game choices.

Survey of Adversaries: In anticipation of cutthroat matches, groups concentrate on their rivals. They investigate their playstyles, inclinations, and systems to foster countermeasures and expect their activities.

8. **Trust and Responsibility**

   Trust is a center part of effective collaboration. Colleagues should trust each other's judgment and direction. Trust guarantees that players can depend on their partners to execute systems, make plays, and satisfy their jobs successfully.

   Responsibility is one more fundamental figure collaboration. Players should get a sense of ownership with their activities and choices, whether positive or negative. Responsibility cultivates a culture of personal development and guarantees that errors are gained from and not rehashed.

   Besides, helpful criticism and evaluate assume a part in responsibility. Players ought to feel happy with giving and getting input from their partners and instructing staff. Useful criticism assists players with distinguishing regions for development and prompts more viable cooperation.

9. **Initiative and Shot-Calling**

   Initiative is urgent to a group's prosperity. Groups frequently assign shot-guests, people answerable for going with in-game choices and planning plays. The shot-guest is a vital figure in driving the group, coordinating procedures, and passing on data during matches.

   Successful shot-calling depends areas of strength for on information, relational abilities, and a comprehension of the group's systems. The shot-guest frequently pursues basic choices, for example, when to connect with the adversary, when to start group battles, and when to withdraw. Their capacity to make speedy, very much educated choices can be the contrast among triumph and rout.

   Authority stretches out past the shot-guest, as players frequently take on positions of authority in view of their experience and in-game mastery. Initiative characteristics incorporate directing and supporting partners, setting a positive model, and keeping a cool head under tension.

10. **Variety and Inclusivity**

Variety and inclusivity are progressively perceived as significant elements in building effective esports groups. Groups that embrace variety benefit from a scope of viewpoints, encounters, and abilities. Inclusivity guarantees that each colleague is esteemed and can add to the group's prosperity.

3.2 Team owners, coaches, and managers

In the realm of esports, group proprietors, mentors, and supervisors are crucial figures who assume essential parts in the achievement and manageability of expert groups. These people are answerable for different parts of group the board, including enrollment, key preparation, player improvement, and authoritative capabilities. This part investigates the meaning of group proprietors, mentors, and administrators in esports, featuring their obligations, commitments, and the effect they have on the cutthroat gaming biological system.

Group Proprietors: The Foundation of Esports Associations

Group proprietors are the main thrust behind esports associations. They are many times liable for the creation, the board, and monetary manageability of expert esports groups. Group proprietors assume a vital part in molding the character and outcome of their associations.

Venture and Monetary Sponsorship: Group proprietors give the monetary support important to lay out and keep an expert esports group. This monetary speculation incorporates player pay rates, training and care staff compensations, travel costs, practice offices, and cooperation in competitions. Group proprietors are fundamental in guaranteeing that the group has the assets expected to contend at the most significant level.

Marking and Promoting: Group proprietors are liable for marking and showcasing their associations. They make a visual character, group name, and logo, which become an indispensable piece of the group's picture. Viable marking is basic in drawing in fans, backers, and financial backers.

Sponsorship and Income Age: Group proprietors effectively look for sponsorships, associations, and supports that can give extra wellsprings of income. These monetary arrangements frequently include marking in group shirts, content coordinated efforts, and special exercises. Sponsorships are a life saver for esports associations, permitting them to help their groups and players.

Player Enlistment and Maintenance: Group proprietors administer the enrollment of players, settling on key conclusions about list changes, contract augmentations, and moves. They work intimately with mentors and supervisors to distinguish and get ability that lines up with the group's objectives and techniques. Fruitful player enlistment is basic to the group's seriousness.

Vital Bearing: Group proprietors set the essential heading for their associations. They arrive at conclusions about which esports titles their groups will contend in, association cooperation, and the degree of buy in different gaming scenes. Vital decisions can essentially affect an association's prosperity and life span.

Managerial Capabilities: Group proprietors handle different authoritative capabilities, including legitimate issues, contract exchanges, and hierarchical construction. They guarantee that the association follows association guidelines and keeps an expert and moral norm.

Maintainability: Supportability is a huge worry for group proprietors. They should guarantee that their associations are monetarily practical in the long haul. This might include expanding income streams, investigating marketing open doors, and overseeing costs successfully.

Mentors: Directing and Creating Players

Mentors are fundamental individuals from esports groups, liable for the turn of events and improvement of players. Their job stretches out past in-game methodologies to incorporate mental planning, group elements, and player development. Mentors are crucial in raising a group's exhibition and upper hand.

Game Information: Mentors have profound information on the games their groups contend in. They grasp game mechanics, character capacities, systems, and in-game strategies. This information permits them to foster powerful techniques and assist players with grasping the subtleties of their individual games.

Procedure Improvement: Mentors work with players to devise methodologies that suit the group's targets. They dissect adversaries, distinguish qualities and shortcomings, and make playbooks that guide the group's in-game choices. Mentors assume a key part in deciding the general procedure utilized by the group.

Player Advancement: Mentors are liable for the singular improvement of players. They assist players with working on their mechanical abilities, navigation, and in-game judgment. Mentors recognize regions for development and give direction and preparing to improve players' exhibition.

Mental Training: Mental instructing is a vital part of a mentor's job. Mentors assist players with overseeing pressure, nervousness, and tension during serious matches. Procedures like representation, care, and stress the board are utilized to upgrade mental flexibility.

Correspondence: Mentors aid the improvement of powerful correspondence among players. They support open and valuable correspondence, assisting players with sharing data, systems, and criticism. Powerful correspondence is fundamental for fruitful group elements.

Group Elements: Mentors encourage positive group elements and collaboration. They participate in group building works out, establish a cooperative climate, and energize brotherhood among players. Mentors expect to make a durable and roused group.

In-Game Direction: Mentors give constant direction during matches. They might go about as shot-guests or give counsel on in-game choices. Mentors help players settle on speedy and informed choices during quick moving interactivity.

Survey and Investigation: Post-match examination is an essential part of a mentor's job. Mentors audit ongoing interaction film with players, analyzing their presentation and recognizing regions for development. This investigation adds to player improvement and by and large group development.

Vital Variation: Mentors assume a key part in adjusting the group's techniques and strategies. They screen the advancing metagame, adversary systems, and game updates, making fundamental acclimations to keep up with intensity.

Chiefs: In the background Administration

Group chiefs are the in the background heads of esports associations. They handle different authoritative and strategic capabilities, permitting players and mentors to zero in on ongoing interaction and readiness. Administrators are basic to the smooth activity of groups and guarantee that they can contend at their best.

Coordinated operations and Planning: Group chiefs supervise strategies and booking. They are liable for movement courses of action, facilities, competition support, practice timetables, and player prosperity during occasions. Chiefs guarantee that players have all that they need to contend easily and actually.

Contract Discussions: Supervisors handle contract exchanges, both for players and backers. They work intimately with group proprietors to get player agreements, expansions, and moves. Supervisors likewise arrange sponsorship arrangements and supports that benefit the association.

Liaising with Competition Coordinators: Administrators go about as contacts between the association and competition coordinators. They guarantee that groups get essential data, comply to competition guidelines, and are ready for contest. Directors work with a smooth encounter for groups during occasions.

Group Correspondence: Supervisors assume a part in group correspondence. They pass on data, timetables, and updates to players and instructing staff. Compelling correspondence guarantees that everybody knows about significant subtleties and changes.

Authoritative Help: Supervisors offer regulatory help, which might incorporate dealing with administrative work, visa applications, and lawful issues. They guarantee that the group consents to association guidelines and keeps up with amazing skill in all parts of their tasks.

Player Government assistance: Player government assistance is really important for group administrators. They address player needs, concerns, and prosperity. Administrators frequently assist players with individual matters and guarantee that their psychological and actual wellbeing are dealt with during contests.

Exploring and Enrollment: now and again, group directors take part in player exploring and enlistment. They might help with recognizing ability, organizing tryouts, and assessing expected initiates.

Local area Commitment: Group directors frequently supervise local area commitment and fan relations. They cooperate with fans, coordinate fan occasions, and assist with building the group's presence inside the gaming local area.

Marketing and Product: Some group administrators are engaged with promoting and stock coordination. They work on the plan, creation, and conveyance of group stock, like pullovers, attire, and adornments.

Supportability and Tasks: Administrators add to the general manageability and activities of the association. They mean to guarantee that the group is monetarily suitable and that all parts of the association run as expected.

Joint effort and Cooperative energy: The Way to Progress

Group proprietors, mentors, and chiefs work cooperatively to make a fruitful esports group. Each assumes an exceptional part, yet their collaboration is fundamental for the group's presentation and life span.

Group proprietors give the monetary support, key bearing, and marking that shape the association. Mentors guide players' turn of events, think up compelling systems, and encourage positive group elements. Chiefs handle the managerial and strategic capabilities, guaranteeing that players and mentors can zero in on their ongoing interaction.

The cooperation among these jobs is vital for making group progress. As esports proceeds to develop and develop, the devotion of group proprietors, mentors, and directors stays a main thrust behind the business' development. Their responsibility and commitments have impelled esports into a worldwide peculiarity, exhibiting the impressive skill, ability, and serious soul of the gaming scene.

3.3 Success stories and strategies for team building

Outcome in esports is much of the time the aftereffect of successful group working, as the collaboration among players and staff is basic to accomplishing triumph. Various esports groups have ascended to conspicuousness through essential group building, and their examples of overcoming adversity offer important bits of knowledge into the techniques and procedures that lead to triumph in cutthroat gaming. This segment investigates a portion of these examples of overcoming adversity and the systems utilized by groups to fabricate winning lists.

1. **Example of overcoming adversity: OG in Dota 2**

OG is a champion illustration of a group that made exceptional progress through compelling group working in Dota 2. OG left a mark on the world by winning The Global, Dota 2's most esteemed competition, not once yet two times in 2018 and 2019.

Procedures for Group Building:

1. **Player Enlistment and Science:**
   OG grasped the significance of player science. They consolidated experienced players with particular playing styles and youthful gifts to make a balanced program. This mix of ranges of abilities permitted OG to be flexible in their interactivity and adjust to different in-game circumstances.
2. **Steady Program:**
   One of OG's key systems was keeping a reliable list. This congruity permitted players to foster solid bonds and a comprehension of one another's ongoing interaction styles, prompting compelling coordination in matches.
3. **Player Strengthening:**
   OG gave players more independence and urged them to be effectively associated with group direction. This player strengthening prompted a feeling of pride and a pledge to aggregate achievement.
4. **Versatility and Outlook:**

OG showed a strong outlook, frequently getting back in the game in high-pressure circumstances. This psychological grit was encouraged through rehearses like care and perception, which assisted players with dealing with the profound and mental difficulties of rivalry.

2. Example of overcoming adversity: San Francisco Shock in Overwatch

The San Francisco Shock is a great representation of a fruitful Overwatch Association group that successfully fabricated a triumphant list.

Methodologies for Group Building:

1. **Vital Enrollment:**
   The Shock put resources into a mix of experienced players and arising gifts. By decisively selecting players who succeeded in their separate jobs, the group made an even program.
2. **Training and Improvement:**
   Powerful training assumed a pivotal part in the Shock's prosperity. Their instructing staff, including lead trainer Dry, executed an organized and information driven way to deal with player improvement, making a culture of constant improvement.
3. **Correspondence and Cooperation:**
   The Shock underlined correspondence and cooperation. They embraced a proactive way to deal with correspondence during matches and scrims, guaranteeing that players were continually organizing and sharing data.
4. **Versatility and Adaptability:**

The Shock exhibited versatility and adaptability by being willing to switch techniques and jobs when required. This adaptability permitted them to answer the developing metagame and counter rivals actually.

3. Example of overcoming adversity: Astralis in Counter-Strike: Worldwide Hostile

Astralis is a prestigious Counter-Strike: Worldwide Hostile (CS:GO) group that made remarkable progress.

Techniques for Group Building:

1. **Information Driven Investigation:**
   Astralis used information driven investigation to assess their presentation. They gathered broad insights to recognize shortcomings, patterns, and amazing open doors for development.
2. **Mental Help:**
   Astralis put resources into sports analysts to assist players with dealing with the mental parts of contest, like pressure, certainty, and concentration. This help supported the players' psychological versatility.
3. **Strategic Greatness:**
   The group was known for its strategic splendor. Astralis zeroed in on careful guide control, utility use, and very much planned methodologies. Their strategic ability put them aside from contenders.
4. **Consistency and Discipline:**

Astralis kept an elevated degree of consistency and discipline in their preparation and execution. They stuck to an organized practice routine and focused on detail.

4. Example of overcoming adversity: SK Telecom T1 in Class of Legends

SK Telecom T1 (SKT) is a predominant power in Class of Legends and one of the best esports groups.

Systems for Group Building:

1. **Player Advancement:**
   SKT put resources into player advancement starting from the earliest stage. Their framework included junior groups, practice offices, and training staff to sustain ability.
2. **Headliner Obtaining:**
   SKT made key acquisitions of headliners who could lead the group to triumph. Players like Faker turned into the essence of the group and pulled in fans and supporters.
3. **Instructing Greatness:**
   The group stressed the job of training. Their instructing staff, drove by lead

trainer Kim "kkOma" Jeong-gyun, formulated very much organized procedures and zeroed in on preparing players to actually execute these techniques.

4. **Strength and Flexibility:**

SKT exhibited versatility by quickly returning from misfortunes and gaining from their mix-ups. They were likewise versatile, making fast changes in light of changes in the cutthroat scene.

5. Example of overcoming adversity: Dallas Fuel in Overwatch Association

The Dallas Fuel, a piece of the Overwatch Association, made progress through a blend of viable group building and hierarchical changes.

Systems for Group Building:

1. **Support Staff Update:**
   The Dallas Fuel rolled out huge improvements to their care staff, getting new mentors, examiners, and a games clinician. This upgrade rejuvenated the group and worked on its presentation.
2. **Player Enrollment and Variety:**
   The group zeroed in on enlistment to construct a balanced list with different ability. They planned to give valuable open doors to players from various foundations, which added to a more grounded and more powerful group.
3. **Fan Commitment:**
   The Dallas Fuel effectively drew in with their fan base. They perceived the significance of making an enthusiastic and committed fan local area, which further reinforced the group's prosperity.
4. **Local area Association:**

The group was associated with local area outreach programs, intending to offer in return and draw in with fans on an individual level.

Key Focal points and Normal Topics:

While every one of these examples of overcoming adversity addresses different esports titles and associations, a few normal topics rise out of their systems for group building:

1. **Player Enrollment:** Compelling group assembling frequently starts with vital player enlistment. Groups plan to track down the right mix of experienced players, arising gifts, and experts in different jobs to make a fair program.
2. **Training and Improvement:** Training staff assume a crucial part in fostering players' abilities, outlook, and strategic comprehension. Organized

training projects and information driven examination are normal techniques for supporting player development.

3. **Correspondence and Cooperation:** Viable correspondence and collaboration are essential. Groups that focus on these perspectives will generally perform well, as coordination and data sharing are basic in serious gaming.
4. **Versatility and Adaptability:** Esports groups should be versatile and adaptable to stay cutthroat. They ought to change systems, jobs, and strategies because of developing metagames and adversary activities.
5. **Mental Versatility:** Groups perceive the significance of mental strength in dealing with pressure and tension during contests. Sports analysts and mental molding programs are progressively normal in esports.
6. **Consistency and Discipline:** Keeping an elevated degree of consistency and discipline in preparing, practice, and execution is a sign of fruitful groups.
7. **Key Vision:** Groups frequently succeed when they have an unmistakable key vision, which incorporates grasping their cutthroat scene and coming to very much educated conclusions about enlistment and game methodology.
8. **Support Staff and Foundation:** Effective groups put resources into help staff and framework to give the important assets to players and instructing staff to flourish.
9. **Local area Commitment:** Building an enthusiastic fan base and drawing in with the esports local area are likewise critical parts of a group's prosperity. Fan backing can make a positive environment that stimulates players.

The Diagram for Progress

The examples of overcoming adversity of esports groups uncover that powerful group building is a multi-layered process that includes vital player enrollment, instructing and improvement, correspondence and cooperation, flexibility, mental versatility, and key vision. The outline for progress in esports consolidates these components to fabricate winning lists and accomplish cutthroat greatness.

As esports proceed to develop and advance, these methodologies and examples of overcoming adversity act as significant illustrations for both hopeful players and associations. The esports business' dynamic nature implies that consistent variation and development are vital to keeping up with outcome in the cutthroat gaming scene. With the right blend of ability, backing, and system, esports groups can try to join the positions of these fruitful associations and transform the universe of cutthroat gaming.

Chapter 4

Triumphs and Struggles

All through the chronicles of mankind's set of experiences, our species has gotten through a bunch of wins and battles. These vital minutes, whether on a worldwide scale or inside the bounds of individual lives, have molded the course of our civilization and the actual quintessence of human life. From the earliest days of our rise as an animal groups to the mechanically progressed universe of the 21st hundred years, our process has been one set apart by strength, development, and resolute assurance.

The narrative of our victories and battles starts with our rise as Homo sapiens, an animal varieties that bit by bit isolated itself from its primate precursors through a blend of hereditary transformations, mental advances, and variation to an influencing world. The victory of bipedalism, which liberated our hands for apparatus use, denoted an early defining moment. The capacity to control objects, construct designs, and style weapons established the groundwork for our predominance over different species. Be that as it may, this freshly discovered strength accompanied its own arrangement of battles as our initial predecessors fought with hunters, unforgiving environments, and the consistent quest for food.

As time went on, we developed into complex agrarian social orders. The disclosure of farming denoted a stupendous victory, as it took into consideration the foundation of settled networks. The development of harvests and taming of creatures prompted surplus food creation, empowering bigger populaces and a shift from roaming ways of life. However, with these farming victories came battles of their own, like the administration of assets, the development of social pecking orders, and the steady danger of starvation and illness.

The victory of the composed word, which considered the safeguarding and transmission of information, was a huge achievement in mankind's set of experiences. From the earliest cuneiform engravings of Mesopotamia to the looks of antiquated China, the capacity to record data guaranteed that the aggregate insight of ages could be gone down through the ages. However, battles endured as data stayed restricted to the people who could peruse and compose, making differences in admittance to information.

The victories and battles of antiquated human advancements are inseparably connected. The ascent and fall of domains, like the Roman, Egyptian, and Inca, showed the levels of human accomplishment and the profundities of our ability for struggle. While these civic establishments abandoned fantastic engineering, workmanship, and social inheritances, they additionally confronted battles like political unsteadiness, outer intrusions, and asset exhaustion.

The victory of the Renaissance, a time of recharged interest in workmanship, science, and culture, introduced another period of human accomplishment. Developments in workmanship, like the utilization of direct viewpoint, achieved an unrest in creative articulation. The improvement of the print machine by Johannes Gutenberg denoted a basic defining moment, as it took into consideration the dispersal of information on a lot more extensive scale. Notwithstanding, the battles of the Renaissance, including strict contentions and social imbalances, filled in as an update that progress is frequently joined by difficulties.

The Edification, with its accentuation on reason, science, and individual freedom, denoted a significant victory in the development of human idea. Masterminds like Voltaire, Rousseau, and Kant tested laid out convictions and established the groundwork for current majority rule governments and basic liberties. However, the battles of this period, including expansionism, subjection, and the proceeded with enslavement of underestimated gatherings, uncovered the pressure between illuminated standards and cruel real factors.

The Modern Upheaval, which started in the late eighteenth hundred years, addressed a huge victory in mankind's set of experiences. It achieved extremist headways in assembling, transportation, and correspondence. Manufacturing plants, steam motors, and railways changed economies and social orders. Be that as it may, the battles of this time were significant also, with the ascent of youngster work, risky working circumstances, and remarkable ecological corruption. The lopsided conveyance of riches and influence led to social developments trying to address these imbalances.

The twentieth century took the stand concerning both unrivaled victories and remarkable battles. The mechanical wonders of the time, from the creation of the plane to the moon arrival, exhibited mankind's unfathomable limit with respect to advancement. Notwithstanding, the century was additionally damaged by the demolition of two universal conflicts, slaughters, and the expansion of atomic weapons. The battle for social liberties, orientation uniformity, and decolonization developments featured the industrious treacheries and imbalances that tormented society.

The victory of the computerized age, which started in the late twentieth hundred years and keeps on forming our present, got with it an upset correspondence, trade, and data access. The web, a worldwide organization interfacing individuals across the planet, has democratized information and opened up additional opportunities for joint effort and development. However, it has likewise brought about new battles, including the disintegration of security, the spread of falsehood, and the advanced separation that passes on numerous without admittance to its advantages.

The difficulties of environmental change pose a potential threat in the 21st 100 years. As industrialization and populace development proceed with unabated, the planet faces an ecological emergency of remarkable extents. The victories of environmentally friendly power innovation and worldwide collaboration in environment arrangements offer expect a supportable future. Notwithstanding, the battles related with progressing away from non-renewable energy sources, relieving the effects of an evolving environment, and tending to the main drivers of ecological corruption are complicated and diverse.

The victory of clinical advances in the 21st hundred years, like the improvement of antibodies and forward leaps in hereditary qualities, can possibly reform medical care and broaden human existence. The battles of medical services access, abberations in clinical therapy, and the moral predicaments encompassing hereditary designing stay major problems. The continuous fight against irresistible sicknesses, as exemplified by the worldwide reaction to the Coronavirus pandemic, highlights the flexibility and versatility of human social orders.

The advanced unrest has likewise led to remarkable victories in the domain of computerized reasoning. Machines are currently equipped for performing complex undertakings, from information examination to independent driving. The potential for computer based intelligence to change ventures and upgrade human abilities is obvious. Be that as it may, the battles related with work removal, moral worries, and the effect on protection and security are wellsprings of continuous discussion and concern.

In the domain of room investigation, the victory of landing people on Mars and wandering further into the universe holds the commitment of new wildernesses and logical revelation. However, the battles of financing, global collaboration, and the moral predicaments presented by potential extraterrestrial life highlight the difficulties of trying the impossible.

The victory of social developments for social liberties, LGBTQ+ freedoms, and orientation equity in the 21st century addresses a huge move toward an additional fair and comprehensive world. These battles have brought about changes parents in law, strategies, and cultural mentalities. By and by, firmly established imbalances and biases persevere, and the battle for equity and value forges ahead with numerous fronts.

In the financial circle, the victory of globalization has prompted more noteworthy interconnectivity and the potential for monetary development. Notwithstanding, the battles related with pay imbalance, monetary unsteadiness, and the effect of globalization on nearby ventures and networks are issues that policymakers and social orders wrestle with.

As we ponder the victories and battles that have described the human excursion, it is clear that our set of experiences is an intricate embroidery woven from both momentous accomplishments and getting through difficulties. It is a demonstration of our versatility, resourcefulness, and assurance as an animal types that we have figured out how to beat innumerable hindrances and keep on pushing the limits of what is conceivable.

At the core of our story is the human soul, a power that has driven us to investigate the profundities of the seas and the immeasurability of room, to make show-stoppers that rise above time, and to fabricate social orders that, at their best, depend on standards of equity and uniformity. This soul has permitted us to win over difficulty, to persist even with overpowering chances, and to make the world a superior spot for people in the future.

However, our process is not even close to finished, and new victories and battles look for us not too far off. The difficulties of the 21st 100 years, from environmental change to man-made brainpower, from medical services variations to civil rights, request our aggregate consideration and activity. It is an update that the tale of wins and battles isn't restricted to the past; it is a continuous story that we are all essential for, and our decisions will shape the parts that follow.

Despite these difficulties, we should draw motivation from the victories of the past and the flexibility of the human soul. We should utilize our insight and innovativeness to address the battles that stand up to us, to manufacture a way toward an additional fair and supportable future. Our capacity to gain from an earlier time, to adjust to evolving conditions, and to cooperate as a worldwide local area will eventually decide the course of our aggregate process.

Wins and battles are the twin motors that drive the human story. They are the yin and yang of our reality, the light and the shadow that characterize our way. As we explore the intricacies of the 21st 100 years and then some, may we keep on commending our victories, gain from our battles, and push ahead with a feeling of direction and assurance, realizing that the human soul is equipped for accomplishing remarkable.

4.1 Tales of victories and defeats

All through the chronicles of history, humankind has been participated in a constant battle for wins and a fight against routs. These accounts, both excellent and private, by and large shape the story of our species and furnish us with priceless examples about versatility, steadiness, and the unstoppable human soul.

Our process starts with the rise of Homo sapiens, an animal groups that remained near the precarious edge of elimination on different occasions. The victory of our initial predecessors was their capacity to adjust and advance, utilizing their insight to make instruments, foster correspondence, and lay out friendly designs. These early victories defeated the cruel difficulties of an evolving climate, hunters, and contest with other primate species.

The ancient victory of horticulture, known as the Neolithic Unrest, was a defining moment in mankind's set of experiences. It denoted the shift from a migrant, agrarian presence to settled rural networks. The development of harvests and the taming of creatures empowered surplus food creation, populace development, and the underpinning of coordinated social orders. However, with this win came battles, including asset the executives, social orders, and the steady danger of starvation and infection.

The victory of composing, a noteworthy achievement in mankind's set of experiences, permitted information to be recorded and communicated across ages. From old cuneiform contents to symbolic representations and ultimately letter sets, the composed word turned into a vehicle for the safeguarding of culture, history, and thoughts. In any case, the battles of lack of education and inconsistent admittance to information made differences among social orders.

The ascent and fall of extraordinary domains, like the Roman Realm and the powerful Egyptian traditions, uncover the glory of human victories in administration, designing, and culture. However, these civic establishments additionally confronted battles, from political unrest to intrusions, asset consumption, and the possible downfall of their power and impact.

The Renaissance, a time of restored interest in craftsmanship, science, and culture, denoted a victory of human imagination. Spearheading specialists and scholars like Leonardo da Vinci and Michelangelo reshaped the imaginative scene, while the improvement of the print machine by Johannes Gutenberg achieved a transformation in information dispersal. Be that as it may, the battles of strict struggles, social imbalance, and the strain among customary and moderate thoughts highlighted the intricacies of this time.

The Edification, a scholarly development of the seventeenth and eighteenth hundreds of years, was a victory of reason, science, and individual freedom. Masterminds like Voltaire, Rousseau, and Kant tested laid out convictions and established the groundwork for present day majority rule governments and common liberties. However, the battles of expansionism, subjugation, and the perseverance of social imbalances exhibited that edification beliefs frequently conflicted with the real factors of the time.

The Modern Unrest, which started in the late eighteenth hundred years, remains as a victory of human development. It achieved earth shattering progressions in assembling, transportation, and correspondence. Industrial facilities, steam motors, and rail lines changed economies and social orders. However, the battles of this time were significant, including kid work, dangerous working circumstances, ecological debasement, and the lopsided conveyance of abundance and power.

The twentieth century was a period set apart by both unmatched victories and uncommon battles. Mechanical accomplishments, from the creation of the plane to the moon arrival, displayed humankind's ability for development. However, the century was likewise defaced by the obliteration of two universal conflicts, destructions, and the multiplication of atomic weapons. The battle for social liberties, orientation correspondence, and decolonization developments featured constant treacheries and disparities inside society.

The computerized age of the 21st century introduced a victory of network and admittance to data. The web, a worldwide organization, democratized information and opened new outskirts for joint effort and development. However, it likewise brought battles, from security worries to falsehood and the computerized partition that passes on numerous without admittance to its advantages.

The difficulties of environmental change pose a potential threat in the 21st 100 years. Industrialization and populace development have sped up the natural emergency. While wins in sustainable power innovation and global participation offer expect a practical future, the battles of progressing away from petroleum products, relieving environment influences, and tending to main drivers of ecological corruption stay mind boggling and dire.

The victory of clinical advances in the 21st hundred years, from immunizations to forward leaps in hereditary qualities, can possibly upset medical services and expand human existence. Be that as it may, the battles of medical services access, differences in clinical therapy, and moral situations encompassing hereditary designing persevere. The continuous fight against irresistible sicknesses, as exemplified by the worldwide reaction to the Coronavirus pandemic, highlights the flexibility and versatility of human social orders.

The computerized transformation has brought about extraordinary victories in man-made brainpower (computer based intelligence). Machines can now perform complex errands, from information examination to independent driving. The potential for computer based intelligence to change businesses and improve human capacities is certain. Yet, the battles of occupation dislodging, moral worries, and the effect on protection and security are subjects of continuous discussion and concern.

Space investigation in the 21st century addresses a victory of human interest and development. The arrival of people on Mars and adventures further into the universe hold the commitment of new wildernesses and logical revelation. However, the battles of financing, worldwide participation, and the moral quandaries presented by potential extraterrestrial life feature the difficulties of trying the impossible.

The victory of social developments for social equality, LGBTQ+ privileges, and orientation fairness addresses a huge move toward an additional equitable and comprehensive world. These battles have brought about changes parents in law, strategies, and cultural mentalities. In any case, well established disparities and biases endure, and the battle for equity and value progresses forward with different fronts.

In the financial circle, the victory of globalization has prompted more prominent interconnectivity and the potential for monetary development. Notwithstanding, the battles related with pay disparity, financial precariousness, and the effect of globalization on neighborhood businesses and networks are issues that policymakers and social orders wrestle with.

As we ponder the stories of triumphs and losses that have portrayed mankind's set of experiences, obviously our story is a complicated account of surprising accomplishments and persevering through difficulties. It is a demonstration of our flexibility, creativity, and assurance as an animal varieties that we have figured out how to defeat endless impediments and keep on pushing the limits of what is conceivable.

At the core of our story is the human soul, a power that has driven us to investigate the profundities of the seas and the boundlessness of room, to make masterpieces that rise above time, and to construct social orders that, at their best, depend on standards of equity and correspondence. This soul has permitted us to win over difficulty, to endure notwithstanding overpowering chances, and to make the world a superior spot for people in the future.

However, our process is not even close to finished, and new stories of triumphs and losses look for us not too far off. The difficulties of the 21st 100 years, from environmental change to man-made brainpower, from medical care abberations to civil rights, request our aggregate consideration and activity. It is an update that the tale of wins and battles isn't restricted to the past; it is a continuous story that we are all essential for, and our decisions will shape the sections that follow.

Notwithstanding these difficulties, we should draw motivation from the victories of the past and the versatility of the human soul. We should utilize our insight and imagination to address the battles that face us, to produce a way toward an additional impartial and maintainable future. Our capacity to gain from an earlier time, to adjust to evolving conditions, and to cooperate as a worldwide local area will eventually decide the course of our aggregate process.

Stories of triumphs and losses are the strings that weave the woven artwork of mankind's set of experiences. They are the accounts of wins that move us and the battles that test our purpose. As we explore the intricacies of the 21st hundred years and then some, may we keep on praising our triumphs, gain from our losses, and push ahead with a feeling of direction and assurance, realizing that the human soul is fit for accomplishing wonderful accomplishments and beating even the most considerable of deterrents.

4.2 The emotional rollercoaster of competitive gaming

Cutthroat gaming, frequently alluded to as esports, has developed from a specialty subculture into a worldwide peculiarity. With a huge number of players and a considerably bigger crowd, it has turned into an extravagant industry. While the emphasis is fundamentally on expertise, system, and cooperation, cutthroat gaming is likewise a universe of extraordinary feelings. Gamers experience a rollercoaster of sentiments that can go from thrill to disappointment, and these close to home excursions are an essential piece of the gaming experience.

In the realm of serious gaming, players are many times taking a stab at a certain something: triumph. The flavor of win is amazingly sweet, and the surge of adrenaline that accompanies winning is perhaps of the most impressive and positive feeling in the gaming scene. Whether it's catching the foe banner in a first-individual shooter or getting the last kill in a fight royale, the euphoria of triumph is a widespread inclination for gamers. It's a snapshot of greatness, an approval of expertise, and a demonstration of the incalculable long stretches of training.

Nonetheless, the way to triumph is full of deterrents, and for each victorious second, there are innumerable losses. Serious gaming is, in numerous ways, an excursion through a scene of disappointments and difficulties. Losing a match, particularly in a high-stakes rivalry, can be a discouraging encounter. The aggravation of rout is much of the time escalated by the acknowledgment that, seemingly out of the blue, a misstep was made, a procedure misjudged, or a shot missed. This feeling of moral obligation regarding disappointment can prompt a scope of gloomy feelings, including outrage, dissatisfaction, and self-question.

One of the most striking parts of serious gaming is the close to home power that goes with the job. Gamers can go from celebration to surrender right away. In group based games, the sensation of allowing down one's colleagues to can especially challenge. The profound rollercoaster that players ride during a match is something that outcasts could battle to comprehend. Nonetheless, for those in the gaming local area, it's a vital part of the experience.

A typical profound obstacle for gamers is slant. Slant alludes to a perspective where a player's feelings overpower their capacity to think soundly and use sound judgment. It frequently follows a series of misfortunes or an especially disappointing loss. At the point when a player is on slant, their interactivity can endure essentially. They could pursue rash choices, face superfluous challenges, or lose center. The idea of slant is like what competitors experience when they're in a "droop," however in gaming, the close to home perspective is in many cases more articulated because of the intelligent and cutthroat nature of the medium.

The feelings experienced during cutthroat gaming are not restricted to triumph and overcome. The gaming scene is likewise home to a great many relational encounters. For example, shaping associations with colleagues can prompt sensations of fellowship and companionship.

Numerous gamers have produced profound and enduring bonds with people they've met online while playing. These connections can be a wellspring of daily reassurance and association, likened to kinships framed in some other social setting.

On the other side, there are pessimistic relational encounters too. Web based gaming networks can be hotbeds of harmfulness, where players participate in oppressive way of behaving, provocation, or savaging. Experiences with harmful players can prompt sensations of disappointment, outrage, and a feeling of weakness. For the vast majority, exploring the social elements of the gaming scene can be essentially as genuinely testing as the ongoing interaction itself.

Perhaps of the main personal test in aggressive gaming is the issue of burnout. Numerous expert gamers practice for quite a long time, contending in different competitions, and streaming their ongoing interaction for huge crowds. The strain to perform reliably at a significant level can prompt mental and profound fatigue. Burnout in esports is a perceived peculiarity, and it frequently requires having some time off from the cutthroat scene to re-energize and recuperate. The close to home cost of burnout can be significant, prompting sensations of aloofness, despondency, and tension.

The peculiarity of esports-related wounds adds one more layer of profound intricacy. The stress on wrists, hands, and shoulders because of dull movements, for example, clicking a mouse or squeezing keys, can prompt actual torment and uneasiness. These actual battles can intensify personal difficulties, as players wrestle with the apprehension about wounds risking their professions or enthusiasm for gaming.

The gaming local area has begun to address psychological well-being and close to home prosperity lately. Associations like "Take This" have given assets and backing to gamers managing personal difficulties. The conversation of psychological wellness in the gaming scene has become more open, assisting with decreasing the shame encompassing these issues and giving a space to players to look for help when required.

Positive feelings are likewise an essential piece of the cutthroat gaming scene. The adventure of making a grasp play, the energy of a very much organized group move, and the delight of outfoxing a rival all add to the close to home wealth of the gaming experience. These snapshots of win and fulfillment make gamers want more and more, even despite losses and mishaps.

In the realm of serious gaming, individual execution is frequently examined and studied. The strain to reliably perform at an undeniable level can be sincerely burdening, prompting sensations of nervousness and self-question. Gamers frequently wind up wrestling with an inability to acknowledge success, a peculiarity in which people question their achievements and dread being uncovered as cheats. This mental test can be especially articulated in the realm of esports, where examination is high and assumptions are gigantic.

Past the singular level, group elements in cutthroat gaming can be genuinely mind boggling. While triumphs with a group can be unquestionably fulfilling, conflicts and clashes among colleagues are normal. Conflicts over procedure, correspondence, or in-game choices can prompt pressure and close to home strain. Fruitful groups frequently concentrate on group building activities and correspondence preparing to really explore these difficulties.

The close to home scene of serious gaming isn't restricted to the singular players and groups; it stretches out to the more extensive gaming local area. Onlookers who watch serious matches likewise experience a scope of feelings. The thrill of seeing a grasp play or a longshot group win can be similarly basically as extraordinary as the feelings felt by the actual players. For fans, esports occasions can be a wellspring of energy, pride, and even motivation.

Regardless of the close to home rollercoaster that is cutthroat gaming, numerous players and fans view the experience as profoundly fulfilling. The ups and downs, the triumphs and losses, are all important for what makes cutthroat gaming so captivating. The close to home venture that players and fans put into the games they love is a demonstration of the force of the medium to inspire significant sentiments and associations.

The accounts of expert gamers frequently feature the profound excursion they set out on. The story circular segment of a player's profession can be overflowing with promising and less promising times. The victory of winning a significant competition, the pain of missing the mark in a urgent match, the strain to perform reliably, and the difficulties of adjusting the requests of the cutthroat scene with individual life are all essential for the profound story of an expert gamer.

Numerous expert gamers have become well known people, and their profound encounters are in many cases in plain view for a worldwide crowd. They manage not just the ups and downs of serious play yet in addition the examination and assumptions for fans. The close to home cost of this degree of perceivability can be impressive, prompting burnout, stress, and tension.

The profound excursion of an expert gamer is likewise impacted by the monetary and vocation vulnerabilities of the business. The scene of esports is profoundly serious, and numerous players confront the consistent apprehension about retirement or assignment. The nervousness over the supportability of a gaming profession can be sincerely burdening, in any event, for the best players.

While the close to home rollercoaster of serious gaming can be testing, likewise a demonstration of the significant effect gaming can have on people and networks. The common encounters of win and rout, the brotherhood among partners, and the energy of contest make a special and sincerely rich subculture inside the gaming scene.

The close to home encounters of cutthroat gaming, both positive and pessimistic, have led to another comprehension of the significance of profound prosperity in the gaming local area. The acknowledgment of burnout, an inability to embrace success, and other personal difficulties has prompted drives pointed toward offering help and assets for players and fans. Esports associations, game designers, and networks are progressively recognizing the close to home parts of gaming and endeavoring to establish a more comprehensive and strong climate.

4.3 Overcoming challenges in the pursuit of excellence

The quest for greatness is an excursion that frequently includes defeating a heap of difficulties. Whether in self-improvement, proficient accomplishment, or some other undertaking, the way to greatness is seldom a smooth one. It is set apart by deterrents, mishaps, and snapshots of uncertainty. Nonetheless, it is exactly in defeating these difficulties that people and networks find their actual potential and push the limits of what is conceivable.

At the core of the quest for greatness is the craving to accomplish one's most elevated potential, to be one's best self, or to arrive at the zenith of a picked field. This yearning is an essential part of human instinct, and it drives people to take a stab at significance in their separate spaces. Whether it's in sports, expressions, science, or some other discipline, the quest for greatness is a widespread and binding together subject.

Be that as it may, the way to greatness is definitely not a straight line; it's more much the same as a winding and frequently slippery way. One of the essential difficulties in this excursion is the feeling of dread toward disappointment. Greatness requires facing challenges, pushing limits, and wandering into the unexplored world. However, with these dangers comes the chance of disappointment, which can be a deadening trepidation for some. The anxiety toward fizzling can smother imagination, limit desire, and keep people from arriving at their maximum capacity.

Defeating the anxiety toward disappointment is an essential step on the way to greatness. It requires a change in outlook, perceiving that disappointment isn't an objective however a piece of the excursion. Disappointments are important opportunities for growth that give understanding, strength, and the chance to develop. As a matter of fact, a significant number of the world's most achieved people have confronted various disappointments en route to greatness, and it was their capacity to gain from these misfortunes that eventually impelled them forward.

One more critical test chasing after greatness is the interest for consistency and commitment. Accomplishing greatness in any field requires a degree of responsibility and teach that can overpower. It implies appearing many days, working on, improving abilities, and making progress toward dominance. Whether it's a competitor preparing enthusiastically, a performer rehearsing for quite a long time, or a researcher directing various investigations, the interest for consistency and commitment is an impressive deterrent.

To beat this test, people should track down inherent inspiration that drives their enthusiasm and fills their commitment. It's the adoration for what they do, the feeling of direction, and the fulfillment of gradual advancement that pushes them along. Accomplishing greatness frequently includes separating long haul objectives into more modest, sensible advances and keeping up with center around the quick main job, as opposed to being overpowered by the tremendousness of the general goal.

Using time productively is one more key component chasing after greatness. Adjusting the requests of day to day existence, work, and different responsibilities with the quest for greatness can be a critical test. Numerous people end up wrestling with the contending requests of profession, family, and individual objectives. Carving out the opportunity to put resources into the essential practice, study, or preparing is a battle that should be survived.

Viable using time productively includes defining boundaries, making a timetable that lines up with one's objectives, and figuring out how to express no to interruptions and exercises that don't add to the quest for greatness. Using time effectively is an expertise that can be created and refined, and it's a basic part of accomplishing greatness in any undertaking.

Perhaps of the most overwhelming test chasing after greatness is the presence of self-question. The pestering internal voice that questions one's capacities, value, or potential can be a strong obstruction to advance. Self-question frequently emerges even with difficulties, analysis, or while contrasting oneself with other people who have accomplished greatness.

Conquering self-question requires building fearlessness and a faith in one's capacities. It includes perceiving that everybody has their own special process, and correlation with others is frequently counterproductive. Encircling oneself with a steady organization of tutors, mentors, and friends can likewise give support and direction in snapshots of self-question. Eventually, the way to greatness requests a faith in oneself and the mental fortitude to deal with self-question directly.

The quest for greatness much of the time includes outer difficulties too. The opposition is frequently wild, and people should endeavor to stand apart among their companions. In reality as we know it where greatness is a sought-after quality, it's fundamental for find a one of a kind point or move toward that separates one. This could include improving, breaking new ground, or carrying a new point of view to a field.

Beating outside difficulties likewise requires strength. The way to greatness is seldom a straight movement; it's more much the same as a rollercoaster with its promising and less promising times. There will be mishaps, dismissals, and snapshots of dissatisfaction. Flexibility is the capacity to return from these difficulties, to gain from them, and to keep up with the assurance to continue to push ahead.

Chasing greatness, dismissal is a typical encounter. Whether it's a dismissal letter from a college, a bombed new employee screening, or a horrible scrutinize, dismissal can be dispiriting and unsettling. Defeating dismissal is a basic part of the excursion to greatness. It requires keeping up with viewpoint, understanding that dismissal isn't an impression of one's worth, and involving it as an impetus for development and improvement.

Analysis is another test that frequently faces those on the way to greatness. While helpful input can be important for development, managing pessimistic or ridiculous analysis can genuinely burden. Beating this challenge includes creating profound strength, the capacity to sift through destructive analysis and utilize productive criticism to improve one's abilities and abilities.

The quest for greatness frequently converges with the requirement for balance between fun and serious activities. Accomplishing greatness can be an all-consuming undertaking, prompting burnout and the disregard of other fundamental parts of life. Finding some kind of harmony between greatness in one's picked field and keeping a satisfying individual life can be a difficult and continuous cycle.

Beating this challenge includes defining clear limits and needs. It implies perceiving the significance of taking care of oneself, keeping up with connections, and supporting one's close to home and mental prosperity. Accomplishing greatness shouldn't come at the expense of generally life fulfillment.

Quite possibly of the main outer test chasing after greatness is the always changing nature of the world. Progressions in innovation, changes in cultural standards, and advancing industry patterns can deliver beforehand fruitful methodologies and abilities out of date. Remaining significant and versatile even with such changes is a continuous test.

Beating this challenge includes a pledge to deep rooted learning. Greatness is certainly not a static state; it is a nonstop excursion. This requires remaining inquisitive, being available to groundbreaking thoughts, and embracing change as a chance for development. The capacity to adjust and flourish in a changing climate is a sign of the people who accomplish greatness.

By and large, the quest for greatness can prompt segregation. The commitment and center expected to succeed in a specific field can at times bring about a feeling of separation from the more extensive local area. Beating this challenge includes tracking down ways of interfacing with similar people who share comparative objectives and interests. Building an encouraging group of people of companions, tutors, and teammates can relieve the sensations of detachment and give significant support and direction.

In certain fields, especially human expression and imaginative undertakings, there is in many cases a strain between the quest for greatness and the requirement for monetary security. Accomplishing greatness may not necessarily in all cases lead to prompt monetary

achievement, and numerous people should offset their imaginative interests with commonsense vocation decisions. Defeating this challenge includes cautious monetary preparation and tracking down ways of supporting one's inventive undertakings without compromising monetary security.

The quest for greatness can be especially requesting in fields that require an elevated degree of practical preparation, like pro athletics or the performing expressions. In these spaces, the body is the instrument, and it is fundamental to keep up with top actual execution. Defeating the actual difficulties of these fields requires thorough preparation, discipline, and a promise to one's wellbeing and prosperity.

A huge test chasing greatness is the strain to reliably keep an elevated degree of execution. Whether it's an expert competitor contending in a progression of games or a performer performing on a requesting visit, the need to convey uncommon outcomes over and over can be genuinely and truly burdening. Beating this challenge requires viable pressure the executives, execution improvement, and procedures for keeping up with prosperity all through the excursion.

The quest for greatness is many times seen as a singular undertaking, however it additionally requires joint effort and participation. In many fields, greatness is accomplished through collaboration, and people should conquer the difficulties of working actually with others. This includes correspondence, compromise, and the capacity to use the qualities of each colleague while moderating shortcomings.

Moral and moral problems can likewise be a test chasing greatness. The strain to succeed can at times lead people to think twice about values or take part in dishonest way of behaving. Beating this challenge includes keeping areas of strength for a compass, moral direction, and a promise to uprightness.

Chapter 5

The Visionaries Behind the Scenes

In the great embroidery of human advancement, visionaries have consistently assumed a vital part. These people have the capacity to see past the present, imagine a more promising time to come, and put into high gear the activities that make their fantasies a reality. While certain visionaries accomplish popularity and acknowledgment in the public eye, many work energetically in the background, their commitments frequently stowed away from view. This paper investigates the universe of the uncelebrated visionaries — the individuals who shape our future without continuously venturing into the spotlight.

The tales of in the background visionaries are however various as they may be moving. They can be tracked down in different fields and spaces, from science and innovation to expressions and culture, from civil rights and compassionate endeavors to business and industry. Their vision frequently rises out of a profound enthusiasm for their picked field and a guarantee to having a constructive outcome on the world.

In the domain of science, endless visionaries have worked discreetly in labs and examination offices to propel how we might interpret the world. These people, driven by interest and a hunger for information, have caused momentous revelations that to have changed our lives.

Frequently turning out steadily for a really long time, they have revealed the mysteries of the universe, made life-saving drugs, and created progressive innovations.

One model is Rosalind Franklin, a physicist and X-beam crystallographer, whose work was instrumental in unraveling the construction of DNA. Her photos of DNA filaments gave urgent proof to the twofold helix construction of the particle. While her commitments were not completely perceived during her lifetime, her work established the groundwork for perhaps of the main forward leap in science.

In the realm of innovation, endless visionaries have driven advancement from the shadows. Architects, software engineers, and creators work resolutely to foster new innovations that change the manner in which we live, work, and convey. These people frequently work in the background, their names not well known, however their creations pervasive.

The tale of Hedy Lamarr, the Hollywood entertainer who likewise co-imagined an early type of spread-range correspondence, is a great representation. Her "recurrence jumping" innovation, made during The Second Great War, laid the foundation for the present remote correspondence advancements. Notwithstanding her critical commitment, her job as a mechanical visionary was to a great extent eclipsed by her profession in media outlets.

In the domain of expressions and culture, visionaries make works that rouse and incite, frequently testing cultural standards and pushing the limits of imaginative articulation. They might stay mysterious or work under nom de plumes, on their specialty as opposed to individual acknowledgment.

Banksy, the tricky road craftsman, is a perfect representation of an unknown visionary whose work difficulties show and dazzles the public creative mind. His provocative and politically charged workmanship has done great things, yet his personality stays a strictly confidential mystery.

Visionaries are likewise at the very front of social change and promotion, working vigorously to resolve major problems in the public eye. They might be grassroots coordinators, advocates for minimized networks, or helpful laborers focused on working on the existences of the most powerless.

Dorothy Day, the prime supporter of the Catholic Specialist Development, is an illustration of a her visionary life to civil rights and pushing for poor people. Her work included laying out soup kitchens, safe houses, and distributions to advance her vision of an all the more and humane society. Her endeavors enlivened endless others to join her goal, and her inheritance lives on in the proceeded with work of the Catholic Specialist Development.

The business world is no more unusual to in the background visionaries who shape ventures, drive monetary development, and improve. While certain business people become easily recognized names, numerous others unobtrusively fabricate organizations, foster items, and lead in their separate fields without the ballyhoo of public acknowledgment.

Steve Wozniak, the fellow benefactor of Macintosh, is a great representation of a visionary whose specialized mastery and developments were fundamental for the progress of the organization. Wozniak's work on the plan of the Mac I and Macintosh II PCs established the groundwork for the individualized computing transformation, yet he frequently stayed in the shadow of Steve Occupations, the organization's charming and public-confronting pioneer.

These models outline the colossal effect of in the background visionaries across different areas. They frequently share normal characteristics, like an enthusiasm for their work, a resolute hard working attitude, and a relentless obligation to their vision. In any case, their accounts likewise feature the difficulties that numerous unrecognized visionaries face, including acknowledgment, subsidizing, and the requests of their work.

Acknowledgment is really difficult for in the background visionaries. While some may not look for the spotlight, the absence of affirmation can be a boundary to subsidizing, joint effort, and more extensive effect. Numerous significant commitments slip by everyone's notice, prompting a feeling of disappointment or unfulfilled potential. The test of acknowledgment features the significance of recognizing and commending crafted by these visionaries.

Subsidizing is one more basic test looked by in the background visionaries. Numerous visionaries, especially those in research, civil rights, or imaginative fields, depend on awards, gifts, or different types of monetary help to seek after their dreams. Getting subsidizing can be a serious and testing process, with many meriting projects going unfunded. The monetary weight of understanding a dream can be a huge hindrance to advance.

The requests of their work are likewise difficult for some visionaries. They frequently work extended periods, face difficulties and impediments, and experience the profound cost of their commitment to their vision. Offsetting work with individual life and taking care of oneself is a consistent battle. The requests can prompt burnout, physical and close to home strain, and a feeling of confinement.

Nonetheless, notwithstanding these difficulties, in the background visionaries proceed to drive forward and make critical commitments to society. Their work is driven by a profound feeling of direction and a pledge to their vision. It is the faith in the significance of their work that keeps them devoted to their objective.

Cooperation and backing are fundamental for the progress of in the background visionaries. Associations with similar people, associations, or tutors can give significant assets and enhance their effect. A steady organization can likewise offer acknowledgment and affirmation of their work, tending to one of the difficulties they frequently face.

Foundations and associations that asset research, social drives, or creative ventures can assume a critical part in supporting in the background visionaries. Giving awards, grants, or associations can assist with lightening the monetary weights they face, empowering them to zero in on their work and rejuvenate their dreams.

Recognizing and commending the commitments of in the background visionaries is similarly significant. Perceiving their work approves their endeavors as well as motivates others to follow their own interests and seek after their dreams. Public acknowledgment can be a strong inspiration and can prompt extra open doors and backing for their work.

The tales of in the background visionaries advise us that development and advance frequently depend on the devotion and enthusiasm of people who work steadily in the background. Their commitments, whether in science, innovation, expressions, civil rights, or business, shape the world in significant ways. The difficulties they face, from acknowledgment to subsidizing, are critical, yet their faithful obligation to their vision drives them to defeat these impediments.

In a world that frequently commends the spotlight, it is fundamental to perceive and praise the visionaries who decide to work in the shadows. Their work, frequently determined by an unflinching confidence in the force of their vision, pushes the limits of what is conceivable and makes the world a superior spot. The overlooked yet truly great individuals and champions who unobtrusively shape our future merit our affirmation, backing, and appreciation.

As we consider the narratives of in the background visionaries, we ought to take motivation from their commitment and assurance. Their work fills in as an update that it isn't generally the quest for individual popularity or acknowledgment that drives progress. All things considered, it is a profound obligation to a dream, an enthusiasm for one's work, and the craving to have a constructive outcome on the world that really matter. The unrecognized visionaries in the background epitomize these qualities and move us to do likewise in our own lives and pursuits.

5.1 The unsung heroes of the e-sports industry

The universe of esports, or serious video gaming, has seen an unprecedented ascent in prevalence and impact lately. With a huge number of players and a considerably bigger crowd, the esports business has developed into an extravagant juggernaut. While the spotlight frequently beams on the expert players and the esports hotshots, there are various unrecognized yet truly great individuals who work indefatigably in the background, contributing altogether to the business' prosperity. These people and jobs, however not generally at the center of attention, are the foundation of esports, and this paper expects to reveal insight into their fundamental commitments.

Esports occasions wouldn't be imaginable without the careful preparation and execution of occasion coordinators. These people work vigorously to guarantee that competitions run as expected, giving a consistent encounter to the two players and watchers. From choosing settings to booking matches, dealing with planned operations, and overseeing innumerable subtleties, occasion coordinators are basic to the progress of esports contests.

Quite possibly of the most noticeable and powerful figure in occasion getting sorted out is Michal Blicharz, the VP of Genius Gaming at ESL. Blicharz plays had a urgent impact in the improvement of esports, with an emphasis on keeping up with high creation norms, proficient player encounters, and top-level rivalry. His work and commitment to the business have added to the professionalization of esports occasions.

Notwithstanding occasion coordinators, a vital gathering of people that frequently slips through the cracks is the creation team. These devoted experts are liable for carrying the fervor of esports rivalries to crowds around the world. They work in the background, overseeing cameras, coordinating transmissions, dealing with specialized viewpoints, and guaranteeing that each snapshot of the opposition is caught and sent consistently to fans.

Game Chief Jeff Kaplan, known for his work on Overwatch, is a praiseworthy figure in the gaming business. While not piece of the esports creation group, his commitments to the plan of esports-accommodating games have made him an uncelebrated yet truly great individual. Overwatch, with its extraordinary characters, different systems, and group situated ongoing interaction, has turned into a foundation of the esports scene, offering invigorating survey encounters for fans.

Mentors and examiners assume a crucial part in the progress of esports groups. Mentors give direction, methodology, and everyday reassurance to players, assisting them with performing at their best. Experts, then again, analyze game information, giving significant bits of knowledge that shape a group's strategies and independent direction. While the accomplishments of expert players are commended, their mentors and examiners frequently work in the background to drive their prosperity.

Numerous esports associations have mentors and experts who work energetically to assist their groups with accomplishing significance. Figures like Kim "kkOma" Jeong-gyun, the previous lead trainer of T1 in Class of Legends, have made huge commitments. kkOma's authority and training style drove T1 to different big showdowns, underlining the significance of the instructing staff in an esports group's prosperity.

Behind each fruitful esports association is a committed care staff that oversees different parts of the group's tasks. Group administrators, advertisers, advertising experts, and monetary officials all add to the smooth working and development of esports groups. These overlooked yet truly great individuals work tirelessly to get sponsorships, oversee financial plans, handle travel courses of action, and backing players' private and expert necessities.

In the domain of esports reporting, there is a framework of journalists, editors, and content makers who give thorough inclusion of the business. They record the most recent news, dissect game turns of events, interview players, and deal wise discourse on the esports scene. Their work assists fans with remaining educated and drew in with the esports world.

Notable figures like Travis Gafford, a noticeable esports writer and questioner, are instrumental in giving thorough inclusion of the business. Gafford's commitment to his art and his capacity to interface with players and fans have made him a regarded figure in esports reporting.

One of the most basic parts of any esports occasion is the analysis group. Pundits, otherwise called casters, guide watchers through the high speed activity, offering experiences, investigation, and in depth portrayal. These experts should be educated about the game, talented communicators, and ready to keep up with energy and commitment all through the occasion.

Numerous casters have become cherished figures in the esports local area. Anders Blume, known as "Anders," is one such individual, celebrated for his work in games like Counter-Strike: Worldwide Hostile. His discourse has added an additional layer of energy to incalculable matches, improving the review insight for fans all over the planet.

The specialized team answerable for broadcasting esports occasions, including camera administrators, sound designers, and specialized chiefs, guarantees that the live experience is consistent and outwardly enamoring. Without their aptitude, the fervor of esports rivalries wouldn't be actually passed on to crowds.

Notwithstanding those straightforwardly engaged with creation, esports occasions depend vigorously on the help of workers and occasion staff. Chips in frequently work extended periods of time to help with undertakings like player enlistment, swarm the board, and authoritative obligations. Their devotion to the esports local area is significant, guaranteeing that occasions run as expected and effectively.

While game engineers, for example, Snowstorm Amusement and Uproar Games, are perceived for making the esports titles themselves, the endeavors of equilibrium creators, game analyzers, and designers who ceaselessly work to refine and further develop the games frequently slip through the cracks. These people are fundamental in keeping a cutthroat and energizing gaming experience for players and fans.

Balance creators like Greg Road, who dealt with games like Universe of Warcraft and Class of Legends, have fundamentally affected the serious parts of esports titles. Their work to make adjusted ongoing interaction has molded the procedures and strategies that characterize the esports scene.

Esports associations and overseeing bodies assume a basic part in keeping up with the trustworthiness and development of the business. Associations like the Electronic Games Association (ESL) and the Expert Esports Affiliation (PEA) lay out norms, guidelines, and associations that professionalize and legitimize esports contests.

People like Ralf Reichert, the Chief of ESL, have made huge commitments to the development of esports all in all. Reichert's work in coordinating and advancing esports occasions plays had an imperative impact in extending the business and its worldwide reach.

Clinical experts likewise structure a fundamental piece of the esports biological system. Esports players, as conventional competitors, are inclined to wounds and medical problems that require particular consideration. Mentors, physiotherapists, and analysts are in many cases part of esports groups to guarantee the prosperity and maximized execution of players.

In the clinical field, figures like Dr. Levi Harrison, a muscular specialist who has some expertise in esports-related wounds, are attempting to address the novel well-being challenges looked by gamers. Dr. Harrison's aptitude and backing for player wellbeing feature the significance of clinical experts in the esports business.

In the background, there is a developing local area of variety and consideration advocates who work to make the esports business more open and inviting. These people advance orientation fairness, variety, and consideration in a male-ruled industry, endeavoring to establish a climate where all people can flourish.

Figures like Soe Gschwind-Penski, a noticeable esports host and backer for variety, have made huge commitments to the reason. Soe's work to help ladies in esports and support inclusivity sets a model for the business, underlining the significance of variety drives.

The legitimate and administrative parts of the esports business are frequently disregarded yet are essential for its drawn out development. Legitimate experts, including contract legal counselors, protected innovation specialists, and esports-centered lawyers, assist with exploring the complex lawful scene of agreements, sponsorships, and player freedoms.

People like Bryce Blum, an esports lawyer and pioneer behind ESG Regulation, play had an instrumental impact in directing esports associations and players through the legitimate complexities of the business. Blum's work features the significance of lawful experts in shielding the freedoms and interests of those associated with esports.

Esports fans and networks are one more unrecognized part of the business. The energetic, worldwide fan base backings esports through viewership, participation, and commitment. Fans make content, fan workmanship, and fan fiction, adding to the energetic culture encompassing cutthroat gaming.

Crafted by fans and content makers, as Ashley Kang, a regarded esports writer and questioner, adds profundity and wealth to the esports local area. Kang's commitment to covering esports and her capacity to associate with players and fans has made her a compelling figure in the business.

In rundown, the uncelebrated yet truly great individuals of the esports business structure a different and devoted local area that backings, sustains, and drives the outcome of serious gaming. These people, working in the background, contribute altogether to the development, impressive skill, and inclusivity of the business. From occasion coordinators to casters, mentors to legitimate experts, they assume vital parts that frequently go unnoticed.

5.2 Shaping e-sports through innovation and infrastructure

Esports, short for electronic games, has quickly developed from a specialty side interest to a worldwide peculiarity. Serious video gaming currently brags millions players and a considerably bigger crowd, making it one of the quickest developing media outlets. The progress of esports can be credited to many variables, however among the most significant is development in innovation and foundation. This exposition investigates the job of development and foundation in forming the universe of esports.

At the center of esports is the innovation that powers it. The development of esports has been made conceivable by headways in equipment, programming, and web availability. The advancement of strong gaming PCs, high-goal shows, and responsive peripherals has raised the gaming experience higher than ever.

Serious players depend on this state of the art innovation to contend at the most elevated level.

Designs handling units (GPUs) from organizations like NVIDIA and AMD play had a critical impact in pushing the limits of gaming visuals. High revive rate screens, equipped for showing smooth, quick moving activity, have turned into the norm in cutthroat gaming. Fringe makers like Razer, Logitech, and SteelSeries consistently develop with consoles, mice, and headsets intended for esports execution.

The improvement of cloud gaming has additionally extended the scope of esports. Administrations like Google Stadia, NVIDIA GeForce Now, and Microsoft's Venture xCloud empower players to access and mess around over the web, wiping out the requirement for very good quality gaming equipment. This innovation makes esports more open to a more extensive crowd, as players can take part without putting resources into costly hardware.

Furthermore, advancements in gaming motors and physical science reenactments have empowered engineers to make more sensible and vivid encounters. Game titles like Counter-Strike: Worldwide Hostile, Class of Legends, and Dota 2 have become staples in the esports world due to their cutthroat ongoing interaction and a consistent stream of updates and enhancements.

The development of esports is likewise entwined with the advancement of real time stages and administrations. Stages like Jerk, YouTube Gaming, and Facebook Gaming have set out open doors for players to communicate their ongoing interaction to a worldwide crowd. These stages have not just led to another age of content makers yet have likewise become fundamental for the perceivability and adaptation of esports occasions.

The esports business has laid out imaginative associations with customary games substances. These joint efforts have led to new contests and associations. For instance, the organization between the Public Ball Affiliation (NBA) and Take-Two Intelligent has brought about the NBA 2K Association, an esports association including proficient b-ball groups.

The job of framework in molding esports can't be put into words. A dependable and quick web association is a life saver for the two players and watchers. Esports occasions are much of the time broadcast in top quality, and idleness free web based interactivity is significant for serious respectability. The development of fiber-optic web, 5G organizations, and server farms devoted to gaming has worked on the nature of online encounters for players and fans the same.

The worldwide reach of esports is made conceivable by global esports associations and competitions. Associations like the Electronic Games Association (ESL) and the Worldwide Esports Organization (IESF) have attempted to make normalized decides and guidelines that advance fair rivalry and professionalization in the business. These associations additionally have significant competitions and associations, like the Intel Outrageous Bosses (IEM) and the World Electronic Sporting events (WESG).

Framework reaches out to actual scenes and fields devoted to esports. Esports fields, for example, the Esports Field in Las Vegas and the Uproar Games LEC Studio in Berlin, give cutting edge offices for serious play and live crowd commitment. These scenes are furnished with the most recent innovation, including Drove showcases and top notch sound frameworks, to convey a vivid esports experience.

The development of university and school-level esports is one more illustration of how framework has formed the business. Numerous instructive organizations have perceived the worth of esports and have constructed committed gaming offices, permitting understudies to partake in aggressive gaming while at the same time acquiring their certifications. These offices offer a climate where hopeful players can rehearse, contend, and get instructing.

A basic component of the esports framework is the job of supporters and financial backers. Significant brands like Intel, Coca-Cola, and Mercedes-Benz have become engaged with esports, offering monetary help and setting out open doors for players and groups. Their ventures bring permitted esports associations to the table for rewarding agreements to players and put resources into framework enhancements.

Interest in esports likewise stretches out to the development of committed esports arenas. These cutting edge settings, intended to have significant competitions and rivalries, are furnished with the furthest down the line innovation to give an unequaled onlooker experience. The Esports Arena Arlington in Texas and the Esports Field in Los Angeles are instances of such offices.

Advancement and foundation have additionally affected the improvement of esports-related programming and applications. Esports the executives stages like Battlefy and Toornament have worked on the method involved with coordinating and facilitating competitions. Streaming stages like OBS Studio and XSplit have made it simpler for content makers to create top notch communicates.

The development of esports has prompted the rise of esports-centered reporting and content creation. Sites like ESPN Esports, theScore Esports, and Speck Esports give news, investigation, and highlights on the cutthroat gaming scene. Content makers on stages like YouTube and Jerk offer inside and out conversations, guides, and inclusion of esports occasions.

As of late, esports-related new businesses have started to investigate new boondocks. Organizations like PlayVS are creating stages to sort out and oversee esports contests in schools. Others, similar to Manticore Games, are dealing with easy to use instruments for making and sharing custom game encounters. These new companies add to the development and advancement of the esports biological system.

Esports associations and groups have likewise embraced advancement by putting resources into preparing offices and gaming houses. There players live and prepare together, with admittance to the most recent gaming innovation. Preparing offices and gaming houses give a climate to players to foster their abilities and structure solid group bonds.

The job of advancement and foundation in esports stretches out to game improvement itself. Esports-accommodating elements like observer modes, replay frameworks, and hearty cutthroat biological systems are fundamental to the outcome of a game in the esports scene. Engineers proceed to refine and improve these elements to address the issues of players and watchers.

Amazing Games, the engineer of Fortnite, has taken critical steps in coordinating esports-accommodating highlights into their game. The expansion of the Fortnite Inventive mode, which permits players to make custom guides and game modes, has enabled content makers and competition coordinators. The progress of Fortnite's cutthroat scene exhibits the effect of engineer support.

The esports business has likewise profited from developments in the domain of computer generated reality (VR) and expanded reality (AR). VR stages like the Oculus Crack and the HTC Vive offer vivid gaming encounters, and game engineers are investigating the capability of VR in serious gaming. AR has been utilized to improve the onlooker experience, with overlays and data shown during communicates.

One of the main progressions in esports foundation has been the advancement of esports associations. These associations, displayed after conventional games associations, have given an organized and professionalized climate for serious gaming. They offer stable professions for players, a surefire timetable of matches, and significant award pools.

The Overwatch Association, created by Snowstorm Diversion, is a fantastic illustration of an esports association that has had a huge effect. The association highlights city-based groups, making provincial pride and commitment. The Overwatch Association's model has affected different games and associations, reshaping the serious scene.

Esports framework reaches out to the telecom area, where conventional news sources like ESPN and BBC have perceived the worth of serious gaming. These organizations have gained freedoms to communicate esports occasions, carrying them to a more extensive and more different crowd. This openness has added to the standard acknowledgment of esports.

University esports projects and grants have additionally coordinated esports into the school system. Numerous colleges offer grants to capable players, giving them monetary help to proceed with their schooling while at the same time seeking after cutthroat gaming. These projects have formalized esports as a genuine profession way.

The improvement of esports foundation has likewise cultivated profession amazing open doors in non-player jobs. Jobs like mentors, experts, casters, and creation experts have become essential to the progress of esports groups and occasions. This has set out a biological system of open doors for people who are energetic about aggressive gaming however may not be players themselves.

The development of esports has likewise brought about the requirement for emotional well-being experts who have practical experience in esports. Players frequently face the difficulties of stress, tension, and burnout, and advisors and clinicians assume a fundamental part in offering help. This acknowledgment of the emotional well-being parts of esports highlights the business' obligation to the prosperity of players.

The improvement of esports foundation has prompted the making of sports science programs explicitly intended for esports. These projects give training on themes like sustenance, actual wellness, and mental readiness. Esports competitors can now get to assets and preparing like customary competitors, improving their general execution.

In synopsis, development and foundation play had a critical impact in molding the universe of esports. Innovative headways, streaming stages, global associations, committed fields, and speculation have impelled the business' development. Esports-accommodating game highlights and the help of game engineers have added to the outcome of cutthroat gaming titles. Associations, broadcasting bargains, and university programs have professionalized esports and set out new vocation open doors.

As the esports business keeps on growing, it will depend on additional advancement and foundation improvement to keep up with its direction. New advances, expanded openness, and worldwide acknowledgment will characterize the following period of the esports transformation. The proceeded with development of the business is a demonstration of the devotion and energy of all interested parties, from players and designers to coordinators and fans. Esports will stay a dynamic and energizing field, constantly reclassifying the limits of contest and diversion.

5.3 Interviews with key figures in e-sports management

While I can't give real meetings, I can reproduce interviews in view of the jobs and points of view of key figures in esports the board, revealing insight into their encounters and bits of knowledge.

Interview 1: The Occasion Coordinator

Questioner: Might you at any point kindly present yourself and your job in the esports business?

Coordinator: obviously, I'm Alex. I fill in as an occasion coordinator for one of the major esports associations. My essential job includes arranging, planning, and executing huge scope esports occasions, guaranteeing they run as expected for the two players and crowds.

Questioner: What are a portion of the difficulties you face in coordinating esports occasions?

Coordinator: There are many difficulties. The scale and intricacy of these occasions are monstrous. Planning with groups, supports, broadcast groups, and overseeing calculated components like scene choice, hardware arrangement, and using time effectively are steady difficulties. We go for the gold, however unexpected specialized issues can manifest. Overseeing such surprising obstacles is essential for the gig.

Questioner: How would you see the future of esports occasions?

Coordinator: what's to come looks unquestionably encouraging. Esports is developing at a quick speed, and with that, the occasions are expanding and more expert. I see a pattern towards coordinating more creative innovation into the occasions to upgrade the experience for the two players and observers. Virtual and expanded reality encounters, intuitive components for the crowd, and, surprisingly, more vivid ways of associating with the games are reasonable later on.

Interview 2: The Group Supervisor

Questioner: Might you at any point depict your job as a group director in the esports business?

Group Supervisor: Sure, I'm Jessica, and I function as a group chief for an expert esports association. My essential obligation is to administer the everyday activities of our group, zeroing in on system, player improvement, and guaranteeing the prosperity of our players.

Questioner: What are a few difficulties you face dealing with an esports group?

Group Director: Overseeing characters and assumptions is a huge test. Every player carries remarkable abilities and characters to the group. Offsetting their yearnings with group objectives, guaranteeing they keep a sound balance between fun and serious activities, and offering backing to adapt to the tensions of the business can interest.

Questioner: How would you see the job of a group director developing in the esports scene?

Group Director: As the business professionalizes, the job of a group chief will likewise develop. Group administrators will progressively zero in on the comprehensive advancement of players, from their gaming abilities to their physical and mental prosperity. Organizing with particular mentors, therapists, and nutritionists to enhance player execution will be a vital area of development.

Interview 3: The Esports Columnist

Questioner: What does your job as an esports columnist involve?

Writer: Howdy, I'm Tom. I function as an esports columnist, covering news, occasions, and leading meetings inside the esports business. My responsibility is to give enlightening and drawing in happy that keeps the crowd informed about the most recent happenings in the realm of serious gaming.

Questioner: What are the difficulties you face in covering esports news and occasions?

Writer: One of the difficulties is staying aware of the fast speed of the business. Occasions, player moves, and game updates happen habitually. Guaranteeing precision while rushing to convey news is fundamental. Moreover, exploring the assorted gaming networks and detailing such that requests to various crowd portions can be a test.

Questioner: How would you see esports news coverage advancing before long?

Writer: As esports develops and earns further respect, I accept the interest for top to bottom, excellent inclusion will increment. More particular and analytical news coverage, for example, player profiles, group methodologies, and in the background bits of knowledge, will probably turn out to be more common. Coordinated effort with industry insiders, offering restrictive access, and building further accounts around players and groups will be significant.

Interview 4: The Legitimate Master

Questioner: Could you at any point make sense of your part in the esports business?

Legitimate Master: Howdy, I'm John, and I'm a lawyer gaining practical experience in esports regulation. My job includes exploring the legitimate intricacies of player contracts, sponsorships, licensed innovation privileges, and consistence issues inside the esports scene.

Questioner: What are a portion of the legitimate difficulties you face in esports?

Legitimate Master: One of the huge difficulties is the quickly developing nature of the business. As the scene changes, new lawful issues emerge. Agreements and arrangements should be painstakingly drafted to adjust to the unique idea of esports. Furthermore, guaranteeing the insurance of licensed innovation and relieving likely questions between players, groups, and associations is a steady concern.

Questioner: How would you predict the legitimate part of esports advancing?

Lawful Master: With the development of the business, legitimate viewpoints will turn out to be more modern. As esports turns out to be more standard, I predict an ascent in issues connected with work privileges, permitting, and the guideline of player specialists. Laying out normalized legitimate structures and guidelines well defined for esports will turn out to be progressively significant.

Interview 5: The Sponsorship and Showcasing Director

Questioner: What does your job as a sponsorship and showcasing director include in the esports business?

Promoting Chief: I'm Sarah. I oversee sponsorship and promoting methodologies for an esports association. My essential center is getting associations and making drawing in crusades that associate brands with the esports local area.

Questioner: What difficulties do you experience in getting sponsorships in esports?

Promoting Administrator: One of the difficulties is adjusting brands to the ideal times inside esports. Tracking down an ideal match between a brand and an esports group or occasion is critical for fruitful associations. Persuading likely backers of the worth and reach of the esports crowd can likewise be testing, particularly with the business actually developing and advancing.

Questioner: How would you see the sponsorship and showcasing scene advancing in esports?

Showcasing Supervisor: As the business develops, I expect an expansion in the complexity of sponsorship bargains. Brands will search for additional incorporated and vivid ways of drawing in with the crowd. The shift towards information driven showcasing, customized encounters, and utilizing the force of powerhouses inside the gaming local area will probably turn out to be more common.

These meetings offer bits of knowledge into the assorted jobs and difficulties inside esports the board, each contributing in their direction to the development and professionalization of the business. From occasion coordinators and group supervisors to columnists, legitimate specialists, and showcasing experts, the aggregate endeavors of these key figures are driving the esports scene forward, molding its future, and pushing the limits of cutthroat gaming.

Chapter 6

The E-sports Tournament Phenomenon

E-sports competitions have turned into a worldwide peculiarity, catching the minds of millions of fans and players all over the planet. While conventional games like soccer, b-ball, and football keep on ruling the games scene, the ascent of serious video gaming has made a subculture that is reshaping the manner in which we contemplate sports and diversion. In this paper, we will investigate the beginnings and advancement of e-sports competitions, the financial effect of the business, the players and groups that make it all conceivable, and the difficulties and discussions that go with this quickly developing peculiarity.

E-sports, or electronic games, is a term that includes cutthroat video gaming. Dissimilar to conventional games, which include actual physicality and actual presence, e-sports depend on advanced innovation and online stages. The foundations of e-sports can be followed back to the beginning of video gaming, where players would contend with one another in arcades or on home control center. Games like Pong and Space Intruders gave straightforward, yet elating, rivalry. Notwithstanding, it was only after the last part of the 1990s and mid 2000s that e-sports started to take on a more coordinated and serious structure.

One of the earliest e-sports competitions was the Cyberathlete Proficient Association (CPL), established in 1997. The CPL facilitated rivalries in games like Shudder and Counter-Strike, offering monetary rewards to top players. These early occasions laid the basis for what might

turn into a flourishing industry. As innovation progressed and web based gaming turned out to be more open, e-sports competitions started to fill in ubiquity. The rise of games like StarCraft, Dota 2, and Class of Legends gave a more complicated and vital type of rivalry that spoke to the two players and onlookers.

The ascent of streaming stages like Jerk additionally filled the development of e-sports. Gamers could now communicate their interactivity to a worldwide crowd, permitting fans to watch their #1 players and groups progressively. This change in how e-sports were consumed led to another age of gaming whizzes, who assembled huge followings and pulled in sponsorship bargains. In 2014, Amazon gained Jerk for almost $1 billion, featuring the worth of e-sports content in the advanced age.

E-sports competitions have additionally profited from the association of large companies and customary games associations. Organizations like Intel, Coca-Cola, and Red Bull have become patrons of e-games, infusing huge capital into the business. Customary games groups and proprietors, like the Philadelphia 76ers and the New York Yankees, have put resources into e-sports associations, further legitimizing the business. The arrangement of associations like the Overwatch Association and the Class of Legends Title Series have made organized, diversified e-sports biological systems that look like conventional games associations.

The monetary effect of e-sports has been downright momentous. In 2018, the worldwide e-sports market was assessed to be worth more than $900 million, with projections that it would surpass $1 billion before long. Income streams for e-sports incorporate ticket deals for live occasions, publicizing and sponsorship bargains, media freedoms, stock, and in-game buys. The development of the business has likewise led to an expert framework that incorporates mentors, examiners, and care staff, further reflecting conventional games.

Top e-sports players can procure significant salaries through a blend of competition rewards and support bargains. South Korean StarCraft player Lee "Faker" Sang-hyeok, for instance, is viewed as one of the best e-sports competitors ever. He has brought in large number of dollars in prize cash and sponsorships. Also, Dota 2 player Kuro "KuroKy" Salehi Takhasomi turned into the most noteworthy procuring e-sports player in history in 2019, with all out profit outperforming $5 million. These examples of overcoming adversity have legitimized e-sports as a practical vocation choice for youthful players with fantasies about gaming fame.

E-sports competitions have given open doors to players as well as made positions and vocations for a large number of experts. Game designers, occasion coordinators, telecasters, experts, and columnists all add to the environment. Significant e-games, like The Global for Dota 2 and the Class of Legends Big showdown, have creation esteems that rival those of customary games. The interest for gifted experts in different e-sports-related fields proceeds to develop, and colleges are currently offering degree programs in e-sports the board and creation.

In any case, the quick ascent of e-sports has likewise carried with it a bunch of difficulties and contentions. One of the main worries is the issue of player burnout. The serious preparation regimens and thorough contest timetables can negatively affect players' physical and psychological well-being. Numerous e-sports competitors have detailed encountering pressure, nervousness, and, surprisingly, actual wounds because of their requesting plans. In light of these worries, some e-sports associations and associations have carried out player wellbeing projects and required rest periods to help relieve burnout.

Cheating and match-fixing have likewise tormented the e-sports industry. The internet based nature of cutthroat gaming makes it powerless against hacking, cheating, and dishonest way of behaving. Players and groups have been found utilizing cheats or deliberately losing matches for monetary benefit. The business has needed to put resources into against cheat innovation and lay out severe standards and punishments to keep up with its trustworthiness.

Inclusivity and variety are other major problems in e-sports. By and large, the business has been male-overwhelmed, and ladies and ethnic minorities have confronted separation and provocation. Drives pointed toward advancing variety and consideration have picked up speed as of late, yet there is still work to be finished to make e-sports a seriously inviting and fair space for all.

Betting and its relationship with e-sports have likewise raised concerns. Wagering on e-sports matches has turned into a critical market, and the potential for match-fixing and unlawful betting exercises is a steady danger. Administrative bodies and e-sports associations have been attempting to lay out rules and limitations to battle these issues.

The worldwide idea of e-sports additionally presents difficulties connected with global contest and visas for players venturing out to occasions. The requirement for predictable and fair standards and guidelines across borders is a continuous issue.

Protected innovation privileges in e-sports are another perplexing matter. Game designers own the freedoms to their games, yet players frequently make content, for example, in-game skins and mods, that add to the general e-sports insight. The subject of who possesses and controls these manifestations has prompted legitimate questions and discussions inside the business.

The way e-sports are communicated and consumed has additionally confronted investigation. While streaming stages like Jerk have democratized content creation, they have additionally raised issues connected with copyright and permitting. Decorations in some cases utilize protected music and content without consent, prompting takedown demands and fights in court.

While these difficulties and contentions present genuine dangers to the e-sports industry, they additionally address open doors for development and improvement. E-sports associations, game designers, and administrative bodies are effectively attempting to resolve these issues and establish a more feasible and comprehensive climate for the business to flourish.

Quite possibly of the main achievement in the advancement of e-sports has been the improvement of establishment associations. These associations have carried design and soundness to the business, giving players and groups ensured pay and making a more maintainable model. The Overwatch Association, for instance, works on a city-based establishment framework, similar as conventional games. This approach has made territorial fan bases and create neighborhood interest in e-sports.

The progress of establishment associations has roused different games and associations to investigate comparable models. The Class of Legends Title Series (LCS) has taken on a diversifying framework, with groups addressing different urban communities across North America. This shift has drawn in speculation from conventional games associations, as they see the potential for long haul productivity and development.

The diversifying model has additionally prompted huge changes in player remuneration and treatment. Players in establishment associations are frequently given medical advantages, retirement plans, and compensations that are more steady and serious. This denotes a huge takeoff from the beginning of e-sports, where players frequently depended exclusively on competition rewards and sponsorship bargains.

The arrangement of establishment associations has not just carried security to the e-sports biological system however has likewise prompted expanded amazing skill in group the board. Establishment associations are supposed to give sufficient assets, training staff, and offices for their players, encouraging a culture of greatness and long haul improvement.

Another component adding to the development of e-sports is the availability and reasonableness of gaming. Dissimilar to customary games, which require costly hardware and offices, cutthroat video gaming can be sought after with a generally unobtrusive speculation. Most e-sports competitors need just a strong gaming PC or control center and a web association. This openness has permitted players from different foundations to contend on a level battleground.

E-sports associations and associations are continually developing to make a more maintainable and fair biological system. Drives pointed toward tending to player prosperity, variety, and inclusivity are turning out to be more conspicuous. The business is likewise attempting to lay out clear rules for licensed innovation and legitimate issues to guarantee a fair and straightforward climate for all partners.

The proceeded with development of e-sports will be driven by the energy and devotion of players, fans, and experts. The feeling of local area and having a place that e-sports give is a strong power, and it will keep on bringing individuals from varying backgrounds into the universe of cutthroat gaming.

All in all, the e-sports competition peculiarity has arisen as a worldwide power in the realm of sports and diversion. From its unassuming starting points in arcades and early web based gaming to the monstrous fields and worldwide fan base it appreciates today, e-sports have made considerable progress. With the backing of large companies, establishment associations, and instructive foundations, e-sports are on a direction of development and extension.

Be that as it may, difficulties and debates, for example, player burnout, cheating, variety and inclusivity issues, and the crossing point of e-sports with betting, should be addressed to guarantee the business' drawn out maintainability. The excursion of e-sports is as yet unfurling, and its future is overflowing with potential. As innovation and culture keep on developing, e-sports will adjust and flourish, offering an interesting and convincing type of rivalry and diversion to a steadily developing worldwide crowd.

6.1 From LAN parties to mega-events

The excursion of e-sports from humble LAN gatherings to huge worldwide occasions is an account of development, energy, and the change of a specialty subculture into a standard peculiarity. In this account, we will investigate the beginnings of LAN parties, the development of e-sports, and the variables that have moved it into the domain of uber occasions.

In the beginning of e-sports, LAN (Neighborhood) parties were the focal point of cutthroat gaming. These social occasions permitted players to associate their PCs straightforwardly through a nearby organization and contend in multiplayer games. LAN parties had a grassroots, DIY soul that typified the early e-sports local area's ethos.

The idea of LAN parties follows back to the late twentieth hundred years, while individualized computing and video gaming were going through critical changes. As PCs turned out to be more reasonable and strong, multiplayer gaming took off. Games like Destruction and Shake, which upheld LAN play, were instrumental in promoting these occasions.

LAN parties were commonly coordinated by a little gathering of lovers who leased a space, frequently a nearby public venue or an unfilled stockroom, and welcomed companions and individual gamers to take part. Participants would bring their own PCs, screens, and systems administration gear, making a shoddy field for contest. These occasions were set apart by kinship, extraordinary competitions, and a DIY climate that reflected the beginning of skating or underground rock.

One of the characterizing highlights of LAN parties was the neighborhood association. Gamers could see and cooperate with their rivals face to face, making a zapping climate. Rubbish talk, cordial chat, and the excitement of triumph or rout were completely capable eye to eye. This powerful made LAN parties a close and closely knit local area experience.

The games highlighted at LAN parties were basically first-individual shooters (FPS), like Shudder and Counter-Strike, and constant system games like StarCraft. These games requested accuracy, speedy reflexes, and vital reasoning, pursuing them ideal decisions for serious play. The ubiquity of specific titles frequently resolved the size and size of LAN parties.

As LAN parties got forward movement, they filled in scale and desire. A few occasions pulled in hundreds, on the off chance that not thousands, of members. Prominent LAN parties like QuakeCon, DreamHack, and The Social occasion became amazing in the e-sports world. These occasions included competition contests, sponsorships, and, surprisingly, little monetary rewards for victors.

QuakeCon, held yearly in the US, was one of the earliest and most powerful LAN parties. It praised the Shudder series of games and filled in as a center point for serious Shake players. Over the long run, QuakeCon developed into a grandstand for Tremor as well as other cutthroat games, highlighting board conversations and competitions with significant award cash.

DreamHack, established in Sweden, was another spearheading LAN party that took e-sports higher than ever. Which began as a little assembling in a Swedish school cafeteria in 1994 developed into one of the biggest e-sports and gaming celebrations on the planet. DreamHack's tremendous occasions united a huge number of gamers, and its e-sports competitions offered significant monetary rewards.

The Social affair, facilitated in Norway, was known for its remarkable blend of LAN party, live event, and imaginative expressions gathering. While e-sports assumed a critical part, the occasion likewise displayed computerized craftsmanship, music, and inventiveness. The Get-together was an exemplification of the e-sports local area's different advantages and gifts.

As LAN parties thrived, the e-sports local area was on the cusp of a significant change. The appearance of rapid web, the multiplication of web based gaming stages, and the rise of live streaming would introduce another period for e-sports.

The ascent of internet gaming stages like Battle.net and Steam, alongside gaming consoles like Xbox Live and PlayStation Organization, permitted players to associate and contend online without the requirement for actual LAN parties. This progress to online play made the way for a worldwide crowd and was a vital stage in the development of e-sports.

The approach of live streaming stages, most remarkably Jerk, upset the way e-sports were capable and consumed. Streaming innovation empowered players to communicate their interactivity to a live crowd on the web, eliminating geological obstructions and conceding admittance to fans all over the planet.

Jerk, established in 2011, immediately turned into the prevailing stage for e-sports streaming. Its easy to understand interface, intuitive highlights like live visit, and an extensive variety of content made it an ideal fit for e-sports. Proficient players and content makers tracked down a home on Jerk, and it assumed a critical part in building the vocations of many gaming characters.

Live streaming brought e-sports to the majority and transformed players into famous people. Decorations like Tyler "Ninja" Blevins and Michael "Cover" Grzesiek amassed enormous followings, with a great many watchers checking out watch them play and draw in with their networks. The ascent of these decorations added to the standard acknowledgment of e-sports and opened up new income streams through memberships, gifts, and publicizing.

Live streaming likewise set out a freedom for e-games to contact a more extensive crowd. Significant competitions started telecom their matches and contests on stages like Jerk and YouTube. The expanded perceivability pulled in patrons and promoters, infusing significant capital into the e-sports biological system.

E-sports associations and groups began to take on a more expert design, complete with mentors, investigators, and care staff. Players started to sign agreements and get pay rates, laying out a make vocation way in the business. Establishment associations like the Overwatch Association and the Class of Legends Title Series offered steadiness and consistency, as well as an organized serious climate.

The professionalization of e-sports led to the idea of e-sports competitors. These players leveled up their abilities through thorough preparation regimens, like conventional competitors. They rehearsed for quite a long time, refined their procedures, and broke down rivals to acquire an upper hand. The devotion and responsibility of e-sports competitors were comparable to that of any expert competitor.

As the expert scene of e-sports grew, so did the potential for money and sponsorship bargains. Top e-sports competitors could procure significant livelihoods through a mix of competition rewards, streaming income, and supports. The quest for gaming fame turned into a practical vocation choice, drawing the consideration of youthful players with fantasies about earning enough to pay the bills from gaming.

The business side of e-sports extended also. Large companies, including Intel, Coca-Cola, and Red Bull, started to support e-games and groups. Customary games associations and proprietors entered the e-sports field, putting resources into e-sports associations and associations. The Philadelphia 76ers, for example, obtained Group Dignitas, while the New York Yankees put resources into Reverberation Fox.

The development of establishment associations was a significant second in the development of e-sports. These associations embraced a model like customary games, with groups addressing explicit urban communities or locales. The Overwatch Association, for instance, highlighted city-based establishments from around the world. This approach gave provincial fan bases and created nearby interest, reflecting the construction of customary games associations.

Establishment associations brought monetary strength and long haul benefit to the e-sports biological system. Groups in these associations got ensured pay and had the amazing chance to partake in the association's income. This model pulled in speculation as well as given a stage to groups to fabricate their brands and fan bases.

The presence of conventional games associations and establishments likewise legitimized e-sports according to the more extensive public. The contribution of deeply grounded names in sports conveyed a degree of renown that e-sports had not recently delighted in. This legitimization reached out to financial backers and patrons, who perceived the business as a significant and promising space.

Establishment associations put an accentuation on impressive skill and player prosperity. Groups in these associations were supposed to give assets, training staff, and offices to help their players. Player agreements and remuneration turned out to be more organized and cutthroat, guaranteeing that players got fair compensations and advantages.

The blend of establishment associations, expanded professionalization, and the development of streaming stages prompted a huge increase in the valuation of e-sports associations. Group valuations took off, and financial backers perceived the drawn out capability of the business. E-sports had progressed from a specialty subculture to a serious business opportunity.

One more significant driver of the e-sports peculiarity has been the openness and reasonableness of gaming. Dissimilar to customary games, which require costly hardware and offices, cutthroat video gaming can be sought after with a somewhat unassuming venture. Most e-sports competitors need just a strong gaming PC or control center and a web association. This openness has permitted players from different foundations to contend on a level battleground.

In addition, e-sports have set out open doors for beginner players to change to the expert level. Online qualifiers and open competitions give a pathway to gifted people to really establish themselves and draw in the consideration of expert associations. Games like Fortnite have held open contests with a large number of dollars in prizes, offering an opportunity for hopeful players to break into the scene.

The ascent of e-sports has likewise carried with it another age of fans and onlookers. The survey experience has been changed by streaming stages, which permit fans to watch their #1 players and groups from the solace of their homes. The intuitiveness of streaming, with live talks and commitment with decorations, has made a feeling of local area among e-sports devotees.

E-games are presently routinely facilitated in huge fields and arenas, drawing in live crowds that rival those of conventional games. The energy and environment at these occasions are electric, with fans applauding their number one groups and players. Significant e-games have likewise been coordinated into the programming of customary games organizations, contacting a more extensive crowd and cementing e-sports' situation in the standard.

The global allure of e-sports is one more intriguing part of its development. While customary games like American football and baseball are basically well known in their nations of origin, e-sports rise above borders. Games like Class of Legends and Dota 2 have monstrous followings in areas as different as North America, Europe, China, and South Korea. This worldwide allure has transformed e-sports into a general language that joins individuals from around the world.

Notwithstanding the worldwide idea of e-sports, its capacity to mix various societies and customs is similarly noteworthy. E-sports competitions frequently highlight a different cluster of players from different foundations and identities. This variety can possibly separate social boundaries and encourage understanding among various networks.

As e-sports have filled in prevalence, they have likewise advanced into instructive foundations. Numerous colleges and schools presently offer e-sports grants, permitting understudies to seek after their enthusiasm for gaming while at the same time procuring a degree. These projects frequently have cutthroat groups that address their schools in different e-sports rivalries. Furthermore, understudies can concentrate on subjects connected with e-sports, for example, game plan, e-sports the board, and showcasing.

The instructive combination of e-sports gives authenticity to the business and offers an organized pathway for youthful players to consolidate their scholar and gaming pursuits. Besides, it adds to the improvement of an all the more balanced e-sports biological system, where players, experts, and fans can draw in with the business in different ways.

The effect of e-sports reaches out past the gaming local area and into the domains of advertising and amusement. Significant brands and organizations have perceived the worth of the e-sports crowd, which comprises of a youthful and carefully clever segment. This has prompted a flood in e-sports sponsorships and organizations.

Sponsorship manages e-sports groups and players have become ordinary, with significant brands like Nike, Mercedes-Benz, and Red Bull conforming to the business. This pattern not just offers monetary help to e-sports associations yet in addition helps standard brands interface with a profoundly drawn in crowd.

E-sports has likewise tracked down its direction into customary media and amusement. TV stations have begun telecom e-games, and streaming stages have marked restrictive substance bargains. Notwithstanding live competitions, e-sports narratives and unscripted TV dramas have acquired ubiquity, revealing insight into the lives and excursions of expert players.

The converging of e-sports and diversion has set out new open doors for content makers and narrators. E-sports accounts are rich with show, contentions, and longshot stories that resound with a wide crowd. The potential for e-sports to turn into a staple of media outlets is clear in the development of e-sports-related content on stages like YouTube and Netflix.

The fate of e-sports is loaded up with commitment and fervor. The proceeded with advancement of innovation, including computer generated reality and increased the truth, is supposed to upgrade the e-sports insight. New games and classes will arise, drawing in new ability and widening the extent of the business.

The Olympic Games have likewise investigated the incorporation of e-sports as a decoration occasion, perceiving the authenticity of cutthroat video gaming as a game. While there are still discussions about the similarity of e-sports with customary games, the potential for e-sports to turn into a critical piece of the Olympic program is a demonstration of its developing impact.

E-sports associations and associations are continually developing to make a more supportable and fair biological system. Drives pointed toward tending to player prosperity, variety, and inclusivity are turning out to be more noticeable. The business is likewise attempting to lay out clear rules for licensed innovation and legitimate issues to guarantee a fair and straightforward climate for all partners.

The proceeded with development of e-sports will be driven by the enthusiasm and devotion of players, fans, and experts. The feeling of local area and having a place that e-sports give is a strong power, and it will keep on bringing individuals from varying backgrounds into the universe of cutthroat gaming.

All in all, the excursion of e-sports from LAN gatherings to uber occasions addresses a wonderful change. The business has progressed significantly from its grassroots starting points, developing into a worldwide peculiarity that draws in the consideration of players, fans, financial backers, and standard brands. E-sports have shown their capability to connect social partitions, cultivate inclusivity, and proposition open doors for hopeful players and experts. As innovation and culture keep on developing, e-sports will adjust and flourish, offering a special and convincing type of rivalry and diversion to a steadily developing worldwide crowd.

6.2 The economics of e-sports tournaments

E-sports competitions have developed into an extravagant industry, reshaping the universe of gaming and diversion. With a large number of watchers and developing award pools, e-sports has caught the creative mind of fans and drawn in the consideration of financial backers, patrons, and media organizations. In this article, we will dig into the financial matters of e-sports competitions, investigating the different income streams, the monetary effect in players and groups, and the potential for proceeded with development.

The financial motor driving e-sports competitions is fueled by a few key income streams. These streams have advanced throughout the long term and are basic in supporting the framework of the business. Understanding how these income streams work is fundamental to grasping the monetary scene of e-sports.

One of the most unmistakable wellsprings of income in e-sports competitions is sponsorship and publicizing. Large companies, going from tech monsters like Intel to drink organizations like Red Bull, have perceived the capability of e-sports and are anxious to put resources into this developing industry. Sponsorship arrangements can incorporate logo situation, brand joining, and elite associations. Supports are drawn to e-sports because of its locked in and young crowd, as well as the worldwide reach of significant competitions.

For instance, Intel has been a long-lasting patron of the Intel Outrageous Bosses (IEM), one of the head e-sports competition series. The organization's sponsorship incorporates naming privileges, marking on competition stages, and broad computerized and virtual entertainment presence. Such sponsorship bargains give a huge part of the income expected to coordinate and execute huge scope e-games.

Essentially, Coca-Cola has banded together with the Overwatch Association as its true drink support. This organization remembers for game promoting and co-marked content, as well as giving different Coca-Cola items at association occasions. Sponsorship bargains like this get income as well as add to the general fan insight.

Another fundamental income stream for e-sports competitions is media freedoms and broadcasting. Significant e-games have inked manages telecom companies and computerized stages to communicate their substance to a more extensive crowd. TV stations, like ESPN and Turner Sports, have communicated e-games, further legitimizing the business according to the overall population. Moreover, advanced stages like Jerk and YouTube are essential source for e-sports content, with selective telecom bargains frequently bringing critical charges.

Jerk, specifically, plays had a critical impact in e-sports broadcasting. The stage permits players and associations to stream their ongoing interaction and live competitions to a worldwide crowd. Jerk offers publicizing and membership income sharing projects, with decorations procuring pay in light of the quantity of perspectives and supporters they draw in. Significant e-sports competitions frequently collaborate with Jerk to communicate their occasions, procuring a portion of the promoting income.

Media privileges additionally incorporate selective substance bargains, where stages like Netflix produce e-sports narratives and unscripted TV dramas. The development of e-sports-related content has produced extra income while aiding assemble the story and accounts of the players and groups. These narratives and series offer a chance for customary media organizations to put resources into e-sports.

Ticket deals and product are significant income streams for huge scope e-sports competitions. Live occasions, held in arenas and fields, draw in a huge number of fans who buy passes to watch the contests face to face. The income produced from ticket deals gives a critical piece of the assets expected to coordinate and stage these occasions. Eminent competitions, similar to The Worldwide for Dota 2, have completely filled fields and arenas, contributing significant income.

Stock, for example, group shirts, player signatures, and collectibles, is one more type of revenue for both e-sports associations and occasion coordinators. Fans are anxious to help their number one groups and players by buying product, and this addresses a chance for associations to make marked items that resound with their fan base. Furthermore, in-game buys connected with e-sporting events, like skins and beauty care products, can create significant income, a piece of which is frequently designated to help serious e-sports scenes.

Prize cash, while a significant cost for e-sports competitions, is one more basic piece of the business' financial matters. The charm of winning significant monetary rewards has been a main thrust for players, empowering them to put time and exertion in leveling up their abilities. Competitions frequently dispense a piece of their financial plan to value pools, which draw in the best ability and lift the cutthroat level of the occasions.

The Global, Dota 2's head competition, has been a trailblazer in the utilization of crowdfunding to support prize pools. Valve, the designer of Dota 2, started the Summary crowdfunding framework, where players buy computerized content, and a part of the returns are added to the award pool. In 2021, The Worldwide 10 had an award pool of more than $40 million, most of which came from the Summary framework. This imaginative methodology has been taken on by different games and has turned into a staple of e-sports financing.

Streaming stages and publicizing contribute altogether to the financial aspects of e-sports. Streaming stages like Jerk give a space to players and groups to make content and draw in with their fan base. These stages produce promoting income in light of the quantity of perspectives and commitment levels. Furthermore, sponsors frequently collaborate with e-sports associations and occasions to arrive at the stage's well informed, millennial, and Gen Z crowd.

The outcome of e-sports has set out new vocation open doors for experts. Mentors, investigators, and care staff are currently normal inside e-sports associations. Mentors work with players to refine their abilities, foster systems, and offer mental help. Experts concentrate on the opposition and make information pushed bits of knowledge to acquire a cutthroat brink. Support staff, including physiotherapists and therapists, guarantee player prosperity and execution.

Colleges have perceived the capability of e-sports and proposition degree programs in e-sports the board, advertising, and creation. Understudies can investigate vocations in the e-sports biological system, working for associations, occasion coordinators, and media organizations. This instructive coordination upgrades the authenticity of e-sports as a suitable profession way.

Players themselves can procure significant wages through a blend of competition rewards, streaming income, and sponsorship bargains. E-sports competitors' profit have soar, with top players bringing in great many dollars in prize cash and sponsorships. South Korean StarCraft player Lee "Faker" Sang-hyeok, for instance, is one of the greatest acquiring e-sports competitors, with profit in the large numbers. This degree of pay has laid out e-sports as a feasible vocation decision for youthful players.

The ascent of establishment associations has introduced another period of solidness and construction for e-sports associations. Groups in these associations get ensured pay, share in the association's income, and contend in an organized climate. Establishment associations reflect the model of conventional games, highlighting city-based groups and an ordinary season followed by end of the season games. The Overwatch Association and the Class of Legends Title Series are great representations of fruitful establishment associations.

The establishment model has been instrumental in legitimizing e-sports and drawing in venture from conventional games associations. The inclusion of sports groups like the Philadelphia 76ers and the New York Yankees has added renown and monetary clout to the business. These associations get their skill advertising, fan commitment, and framework, further propelling the e-sports biological system.

The professionalization of e-sports additionally addresses player prosperity and burnout. The extraordinary preparation regimens and thorough contest timetables can negatively affect players' physical and psychological well-being. Associations in establishment associations, alongside administrative bodies, have carried out player wellbeing projects and required rest periods to relieve burnout and defend players' wellbeing.

E-sports associations additionally take part in promoting and marking to reinforce their pay. Fans are anxious to buy group pullovers, stock, and other marked items to show their help. Fruitful marking assists associations with building a steadfast fan base and sell their items. Making serious areas of strength for a character is critical to an association's drawn out monetary achievement.

Regardless of the various income streams and monetary open doors in e-sports, there are difficulties and discussions that the business should wrestle with. Player burnout is a huge worry, with the determined practice and rivalry plans negatively affecting players' physical and emotional well-being. E-sports associations and administrative bodies are attempting to lay out rules and guidelines to moderate burnout, for example, compulsory rest periods and health programs.

Cheating and match-fixing outrages have additionally damaged the standing of e-sports. The cutthroat idea of the business, combined with huge monetary motivators, has driven a few players to take part in exploitative way of behaving. To battle this, e-sports associations and administrative bodies have carried out severe enemy of conning measures, including programming sweeps and rule implementation.

Variety and inclusivity are major problems in e-sports. By and large, e-sports has been male-ruled, and ladies and minimized bunches have confronted hindrances to passage. E-sports associations are effectively attempting to resolve this issue by cultivating inclusivity and setting out open doors for underrepresented people. Drives pointed toward advancing variety and consideration are fundamental for the drawn out development and progress of the business.

The crossing point of e-sports and betting is one more area of concern. Wagering on e-games has become progressively well known, bringing up issues about the potential for match-fixing and underage betting. E-sports associations and administrative bodies are creating rules and guidelines to guarantee fair and straightforward rivalry while protecting the trustworthiness of the business.

The monetary effect of e-sports isn't restricted to the actual business; it reaches out to the more extensive economy. Have urban communities and locales benefit from the convergence of fans, who burn through cash on facilities, feasting, and diversion. E-games have added to neighborhood the travel industry and produced pay for organizations nearby competition scenes.

In the domain of streaming and content creation, e-sports has set out open doors for people to fabricate professions and revenue sources. Well known decorations and content makers acquire income from memberships, gifts, and publicizing. They frequently change from being players to becoming unmistakable characters, using their fan base and commitment to create pay.

The financial aspects of e-sports competitions are not restricted to the present; they likewise hold the potential for future development. The proceeded with advancement of innovation, including computer generated reality and increased the truth, is supposed to upgrade the e-sports insight. New games and classes will arise, drawing in new ability and widening the extent of the business.

The potential for e-sports to turn into a critical piece of the Olympic program is one more road for development. The Olympic Games have investigated the consideration of e-sports as a decoration occasion, perceiving the authenticity of cutthroat video gaming as a game. While there are still discussions about the similarity of e-sports with conventional games, the potential for e-sports to turn into a critical piece of the Olympic program is a demonstration of its developing impact.

E-sports associations and associations are continually developing to make a more manageable and fair biological system. Drives pointed toward tending to player prosperity, variety, and inclusivity are turning out to be more unmistakable. The business is likewise attempting to lay out clear rules for licensed innovation and legitimate issues to guarantee a fair and straightforward climate for all partners.

All in all, the financial matters of e-sports competitions address a perplexing and dynamic scene. E-sports hosts developed from LAN gatherings and limited scope social occasions into an extravagant industry with different income streams. Sponsorships, promoting, media freedoms, ticket deals, product, and prize cash are the mainstays of this biological system. The professionalization of e-sports, the ascent of establishment associations, and the instructive coordination of e-sports have additionally filled its development. Nonetheless, the business faces difficulties, for example, player burnout, cheating, variety and inclusivity issues, and the convergence of e-sports with betting. Notwithstanding these difficulties, the fate of e-sports is promising, with the potential for proceeded with development and financial thriving for all partners included.

6.3 Fan engagement and the evolution of spectatorship

The universe of sports and amusement has been significantly affected by the ascent of e-sports. Past the players and groups, the core of e-sports dwells in its committed and energetic fan base. In this investigation of fan commitment and the advancement of spectatorship, we will analyze how e-sports has changed the connection among fans and the games they love, and how innovation has empowered new and intelligent ways for onlookers to submerge themselves in the e-sports insight.

One of the main attributes of e-sports is the dynamic commitment of its fan base. In contrast to customary games, where onlookers are principally detached watchers, e-avid supporters have the amazing chance to cooperate with the substance they consume. This cooperation is worked with by advanced stages, live streaming, and the intrinsic intelligence of computer games.

At the core of fan commitment in e-sports is the streaming stage, with Jerk being the most prominent. Jerk permits players, content makers, and e-sports associations to communicate their ongoing interaction and rivalries to a worldwide crowd. The live talk highlight on Jerk empowers constant correspondence among decorations and watchers, establishing a climate for guaranteed connection.

Fans on Jerk can buy into their #1 decorations, opening selective acts out, identifications, and admittance to supporter just happy. This membership model gives an immediate kind of revenue for decorations and cultivates a feeling of having a place among their supporter networks. Gifts and tips from watchers further add to the monetary help of content makers, stressing major areas of strength for the among decorations and their fans.

The intelligent idea of Jerk reaches out to e-games too. Significant competitions and associations frequently broadcast their rivalries on the stage, where fans can partake in live visit, draw in with different watchers, and applaud their #1 groups and players. The continuous part of Jerk visit makes a common encounter, much the same as going to a live occasion, in spite of being in the solace of one's home.

One more critical part of fan commitment is the idea of "being a fan." E-avid supporters are known for their faithful devotion to explicit players, groups, and games. They frequently recognize themselves as fanatics of a specific e-sports association, player, or game title, and this connection is a focal piece of their character.

Being a fan in e-sports goes past basically watching games. Fans effectively support their number one players and groups through different means, like buying stock, going to live occasions, and in any event, making fan workmanship and content. They gladly wear group shirts, wave group banners, and game their number one player's in-game skins.

The feeling of having a place with a local area of similar fans is a main trait of e-sports being a fan. This common energy joins fans, cultivates serious areas of strength for an of brotherhood, and fabricates enduring connections. Being a fan isn't restricted by topographical limits; e-sports devotees from around the world can interface and offer their adoration for the games they follow.

The joining of e-sports into computerized culture has led to another type of being a fan: image culture. Images, frequently clever and interesting, are divided between fans to communicate their encounters, feelings, and inside kids about e-sports. These images course via virtual entertainment and in fan networks, filling in as a type of social cash and a way for fans to associate through humor.

Spectatorship in e-sports is set apart by the variety of content and survey encounters accessible to fans. Past live competition communicates, fans can get to a wide exhibit of content, including investigation shows, syndicated programs, and in the background narratives. This assorted substance biological system develops the fan's association with the e-sports world and upgrades how they might interpret the games they follow.

Investigation shows, frequently facilitated by e-sports specialists and previous players, give inside and out bits of knowledge into techniques, ongoing interaction, and player exhibitions. These shows assist fans with fostering a more profound comprehension of the games and the complexities of undeniable level contest. Content like this has made a more instructed and knowing fan base, encouraging an appreciation for the abilities and strategies of expert players.

Syndicated programs, for example, "The Joe Rogan Experience," have included e-sports characters and players as visitors. This hybrid with standard diversion has helped e-sports contact a more extensive crowd and grow its allure. It has likewise empowered e-sports devotees to draw in with their #1 players and characters in an alternate setting.

In the background narratives and unscripted TV dramas offer a brief look into the existences of e-sports experts. These shows furnish fans with a more unique interaction to their number one players, uncovering their battles, goals, and day to day schedules. This close to home association among fans and players upgrades the onlooker experience.

Notwithstanding the assorted substance contributions, innovative progressions have altogether changed the observer experience. Computer generated Reality (VR) and Increased Reality (AR) advances have opened up additional opportunities for fans to drench themselves in e-sports.

VR permits fans to watch games from inside the virtual field, providing them with a feeling of being available at the occasion. They can move around the virtual space, pick different vantage focuses, and even interface with other virtual observers. This innovation upgrades the feeling of presence and permits fans to feel like dynamic members in the occasion.

AR has been utilized to improve the in-person seeing involvement with live occasions. Utilizing AR applications on their cell phones or AR glasses, observers can get to constant insights, player profiles, and expanded designs overlaid on the actual field. AR adds an additional layer of data and commitment for fans in participation.

The e-sports industry has perceived the capability of AR and VR for fan commitment. The ESL One Hamburg 2017 Dota 2 competition, for instance, consolidated VR by permitting fans to encounter the occasion through VR headsets. This creative methodology exhibits the business' obligation to giving interesting and vivid survey encounters.

The development of e-sports into the universe of portable gaming has additionally influenced spectatorship. Portable gaming has its own devoted fan base, and versatile e-sports competitions have acquired ubiquity. Portable games are more open to a more extensive crowd, permitting fans to watch and partake in e-games on their cell phones or tablets.

Observer modes in games like Conflict Royale and Fight Stars have been planned considering fan commitment. These modes permit players to observe live matches and competitions from inside the game client, offering a helpful and incorporated survey insight. Fans can follow their number one players and groups straightforwardly through the games they play.

The idea of "skin economy" has additionally developed fan commitment in e-sports. Skins are corrective things in computer games that change the presence of in-game characters or items. In games like Counter-Strike: Worldwide Hostile (CS:GO) and Class of Legends, fans can buy skins connected with e-sports groups and competitions. A part of the returns from skin deals frequently goes toward supporting the separate groups or occasions.

Skins make an unmistakable and monetarily open way for fans to show their help for e-sports. The capacity to tweak in-game characters with group logos or player marks upgrades the association among fans and the cutthroat scene. Skin economies are likewise a kind of revenue for e-sports associations and occasion coordinators.

The significance of fan commitment reaches out to live occasions. E-sports competitions held in arenas and fields draw great many fans who come to help their #1 players and groups. The energy and climate at these occasions are electric, with fans cheering, reciting, and waving banners. Live occasions give a valuable chance to fans to associate face to face and share their energy for e-sports.

Being a fan stretches out to live occasions, with fans wearing group pullovers, face paint, and other product. They bring standards, banners, and signs to show their help for players and groups. The feeling of solidarity among fans makes a vivid and zapping climate, similar to the enthusiasm of conventional games.

The mix of e-sports into the programming of customary games networks plays had a crucial impact in contacting a more extensive crowd. Significant organizations like ESPN, Turner Sports, and BBC have perceived the capability of e-sports and communicated competitions and contests. This openness has acquainted e-sports with watchers who might not have known all about the business.

The Olympics' investigation of e-sports as a potential decoration occasion has likewise filled its authenticity. While the similarity of e-sports with conventional games is as yet discussed, the consideration of e-sports in the Olympic program connotes the business' developing impact. It makes the way for e-sports earning respect as a genuine game on a worldwide stage.

E-sports has advanced into instructive foundations, offering grant programs and serious groups. Colleges and universities currently give potential open doors to understudies to seek after their enthusiasm for gaming while at the same time procuring a degree. These projects frequently have cutthroat groups that address their schools in different e-sports contests.

The coordination of e-sports into instruction gives an organized pathway to youthful players to join their intellectual and gaming pursuits. Understudies can concentrate on subjects connected with e-sports, for example, game plan, e-sports the board, and advertising. This instructive coordination upgrades the authenticity of e-sports as a feasible vocation way.

Chapter 7

E-sports and Culture

E-sports, short for electronic games, is a social peculiarity that has quickly acquired conspicuousness in the 21st 100 years. It addresses the convergence of computer games, innovation, and cutthroat games, offering a one of a kind type of diversion that has caught the minds of millions all over the planet. In this investigation of E-sports and culture, we will analyze how E-sports has molded and been formed by the more extensive social scene, remembering its effect for workmanship, character, social elements, and even training.

E-sports as Social Articulation

E-sports have arisen as a strong type of social articulation, typifying the combination of gaming and contest. It is a social space where people and networks meet up to participate in a common encounter, not at all like customary games. Inside this social space, members and fans make their own personalities, accounts, and customs.

The meaning of E-sports in this social setting is exemplified by the manner in which it has penetrated standard culture. Significant E-games, like the Class of Legends Big showdown, Dota 2's The Worldwide, and the Overwatch Association Fabulous Finals, draw gigantic worldwide crowds. These occasions are displays of expertise as well as social exhibitions, including amazing opening functions, unrecorded music exhibitions, and elaborate enhanced visualizations. They are not generally bound to the universe of gaming; they are standard comprehensive developments.

E-sports culture is additionally exemplified by the development of E-sports associations and groups. These associations have created special brands, logos, and group societies. For example, Group Fluid is known for its pony themed marking, while the Dallas Fuel of the Overwatch Association addresses the city of Dallas with its intense blue and white variety conspire. These brands have become social images, typifying the personality of the groups and their fans.

Workmanship and E-sports

Creative articulation and E-sports frequently cross in striking ways. This combination of craftsmanship and rivalry is clear in the plan of E-sports fields, the illustrations and special visualizations utilized in communicates, and the game designers' consideration regarding establishing tastefully satisfying gaming conditions.

E-sports fields, where live occasions are held, frequently include state of the art plan components. These spaces are practical as well as outwardly enamoring. The engineering and inside plan are cautiously arranged to make a vivid encounter for both in-person participants and watchers watching on the web. The astonishing Drove shows, elaborate stage arrangements, and lighting impacts are all important for the masterfulness that encompasses E-games.

Besides, the visual parts of E-sports communicates are a vital part of the social experience. Telecasters utilize progressed designs, expanded reality, and outwardly captivating changes to upgrade the watcher's insight. These components are instructive as well as add to the display of E-sports. The masterfulness of broadcasting adds to the social meaning of the occasions.

The actual games, which are at the center of E-sports, are show-stoppers by their own doing. Game engineers put vigorously in making shocking visual plans, complex characters, and many-sided universes. These games are a stage for rivalry as well as a material for creative articulation. Titles like Class of Legends and Overwatch are commended for their creative accomplishments and have gathered followings for their visual narrating.

E-sports likewise motivate fan-made craftsmanship, from fan fiction and fan workmanship to music and cosplay. Excited fans express their inventiveness by delivering content connected with their number one games, groups, and players. This overflow of imaginative articulation further improves E-sports culture.

Character and Inclusivity

E-sports have given a stage to different voices and characters to track down portrayal and acknowledgment. By and large, gaming has frequently been viewed as a male-ruled space, yet E-sports have tested this generalization by cultivating a climate that is more comprehensive and inviting to people, everything being equal.

Ladies in E-sports, for example, have been pushing for more noteworthy perceivability and acknowledgment. Associations and drives like Ladies in Games, as well as female E-sports groups, have arisen to advocate for orientation uniformity in the business. While challenges continue, there is a developing consciousness of the significance of cultivating inclusivity and variety in E-sports.

The LGBTQ+ people group is likewise finding a spot in E-sports. The support for LGBTQ+ freedoms and inclusivity has been embraced by E-sports associations and players, for certain groups partaking in drives like the You Can Play Undertaking, which advances LGBTQ+ inclusivity in sports. E-sports are progressively viewed as an inviting space for people of every sexual direction.

Besides, the ascent of global players and groups has extended the social variety inside E-sports. Games like Dota 2 and Class of Legends draw in players and fans from everywhere the world. E-sports associations field players from different nations, adding to the worldwide and various nature of the business.

Social Elements and Networks

E-sports have brought about lively and closely knit networks. The internet based nature of gaming and E-sports has cultivated a feeling of having a place among fans and players who might be geologically far off however share a typical energy.

The E-sports local area is described by its own language, images, and ceremonies. It has its own legends, its own stories, and its own contentions. This feeling of local area stretches out to online gatherings, virtual entertainment, and E-sports-committed stages like Liquipedia, Dotabuff, or Over.gg, where fans can take part in conversations, break down measurements, and drench themselves in the realm of E-sports.

This web-based fellowship frequently rises above the virtual world, with E-sports aficionados going to live occasions to meet their internet based companions and offer in the fervor of in-person rivalry. E-sports competitions act as a nexus for these networks, giving a space to fans to meet up and commend their common advantages.

The presence of expert players further reinforces the feeling of local area. Players frequently draw in with fans through live streams, web-based entertainment, and fan meet-and-welcomes. These cooperations cause fans to feel more associated with the players and make a feeling of shared appreciation.

Training and E-sports

E-sports have likewise advanced into the instructive scene. Numerous colleges and schools currently offer E-sports grants, permitting understudies to seek after their enthusiasm for gaming while at the same time procuring a degree. These projects frequently have serious groups that address their schools in different E-sports contests.

Schooling in E-sports reaches out past interactivity. Understudies can concentrate on subjects connected with E-sports, for example, game plan, E-sports the board, promoting, and occasion creation. These projects give understudies balanced schooling that sets them up for professions both in and beyond E-sports.

E-sports training offers authenticity to the business and gives an organized pathway to youthful players to consolidate their intellectual and gaming pursuits. It likewise adds to the improvement of an all the more balanced E-sports biological system, where players, experts, and fans can draw in with the business in different ways.

E-sports and Conventional Games

E-sports and conventional games have run into each other in fascinating ways, with the previous earning respect as a genuine brandishing pursuit. The ascent of E-sports has drawn in the consideration of customary games associations and, surprisingly, prompted coordinated efforts between the two universes.

Significant games establishments, like the Philadelphia 76ers, the New York Yankees, and the Brilliant State Champions, have wandered into E-sports proprietorship. They have perceived the capability of E-sports and the common parts of contest, being a fan, and cooperation. The inclusion of conventional games groups has added renown and monetary clout to the E-sports industry.

Also, customary games associations, like the NBA and the NFL, have embraced E-sports by sending off their own E-sports associations. The NBA 2K Association and the Infuriate NFL Title Series are instances of how customary games associations have broadened their venture into the domain of E-sports.

These hybrids between E-sports and conventional games have likewise appeared in live occasions. E-games have been held in conventional games settings, for example, the Staples Community in Los Angeles, Madison Square Nursery in New York, and the Mercedes-Benz Field in Shanghai. This union of scenes features the equals between the two universes and shows the social meaning of E-sports.

E-sports and Music

The universes of E-sports and music have additionally met, with specialists adding to the social scene of E-games. Music exhibitions have turned into a staple of significant E-sports competitions, filling in as diversion during breaks and opening services.

Top craftsmen, groups, and DJs have performed at E-games, increasing the feeling of scene and adding to the social experience. These exhibitions are frequently spilled to a large number of watchers, building up the social meaning of E-sports.

Alternately, E-sports have impacted the music business. Game soundtracks, especially those of famous E-sports titles, have gathered a fan following. Game music writers have earned respect for their commitments to the E-sports insight, further interweaving the two social areas.

E-sports and Writing

The universe of E-sports has tracked down its place in writing, with books and distributions that dig into the business' set of experiences, culture, and stories. E-sports diaries and memoirs of unmistakable players and figures have become famous, offering perusers an inside investigate the lives and encounters of those in the E-sports world.

E-sports reporting has likewise thrived, with devoted authors and distributions covering E-sports news, occasions, and investigation. These distributions furnish fans with a more profound comprehension of the business and its social importance.

In the domain of sci-fi and dream writing, E-sports and computer generated reality have frequently been focal subjects. Creators have investigated the potential outcomes of virtual universes, serious gaming, and the effect of E-sports on society.

These works of fiction mirror the social pertinence of E-sports in the more extensive artistic scene.

E-sports and Streaming

The ascent of streaming stages, especially Jerk, has been instrumental in forming the way of life of E-sports. Streaming has changed E-sports from a specialty subculture into a standard social peculiarity. It has permitted players, content makers, and E-sports associations to communicate their interactivity and competitions to a worldwide crowd.

Jerk, specifically, has turned into a focal center point for E-sports content. Players and content makers utilize the stage to draw in with their fan base, give live analysis, and feature their abilities. The live talk highlight on Jerk empowers continuous correspondence among decorations and watchers, establishing a climate for sure fire association.

Sponsorships and promoting on streaming stages contribute altogether to the monetary wellbeing of E-sports. Large companies, like Intel and Coca-Cola, have perceived the capability of E-sports and put resources into sponsorship manages players, content makers, and competitions. These arrangements are a wellspring of income as well as a sign of the social meaning of E-sports.

Streaming stages have set out new profession open doors in E-sports. Content makers and decorations acquire pay in light of the quantity of perspectives, endorsers, and gifts they draw in. This pay has pursued streaming a practical vocation decision, permitting people to produce income while drawing in with their fan base.

The Fate of E-sports and Culture

The social meaning of E-sports is probably going to keep advancing and growing from now on. As innovation propels, E-sports will probably investigate new wildernesses, including computer generated reality, increased reality, and 5G network. These mechanical improvements will offer new ways for fans to drench themselves in E-sports and further upgrade the observer experience.

The proceeded with development of E-sports grant programs and instructive drives will add to the authenticity of the business and give amazing chances hoping for experts. Training in E-sports will probably differentiate, enveloping a more extensive scope of subjects, from training and sports brain science to occasion the board and game plan.

The convergence of E-sports with conventional games and the standard social scene is supposed to develop. More customary games associations and associations are probably going to put resources into E-sports, while E-games will keep on being held in conventional games scenes. The cooperation between the two universes will additionally support the social meaning of E-sports.

The connection between E-sports and music, writing, and human expressions will probably keep on prospering, with craftsmen and makers finding motivation in the E-sports world. Music exhibitions at E-games will turn out to be considerably more intricate and necessary to the by and large social experience. Moreover, the impact of E-sports on writing and imaginative articulation will probably develop.

The social effect of E-sports on character and inclusivity will be a proceeding with subject. Endeavors to advance variety and inclusivity in the E-sports industry will probably pick up speed, adding to a really inviting and delegate social scene. The narratives of ladies and LGBTQ+ people in E-sports will be additionally enhanced and celebrated.

7.1 E-sports' impact on popular culture

E-sports, the serious universe of video gaming, has encountered a fleeting ascent throughout the course of recent many years. What started as limited scale rivalries among companions has changed into an extravagant industry with a worldwide reach. In this investigation of E-sports' effect on mainstream society, we will dive into how serious gaming has turned into a social juggernaut, impacting the gaming scene as well as music, style, traditional press, and, surprisingly, the manner in which we characterize physicality.

The Development of E-sports

E-sports, short for electronic games, has seen a wonderful development since its commencement. Early rivalries were much of the time nearby undertakings, with companions and little gatherings of devotees going up against one another for the sheer love of gaming. These grassroots rivalries, regularly known as LAN parties, established the groundwork for the serious gaming society that we see today.

The defining moment for E-sports accompanied the appearance of web based gaming and the multiplication of high velocity web. The capacity to rival players from around the world denoted a seismic change in the business. Games like Star-Craft, Counter-Strike, and Warcraft III made ready for the serious gaming scene, with competitions offering significant monetary rewards and acknowledgment.

In South Korea, E-sports took on an especially huge social job. The country's energy for cutthroat gaming, especially games like StarCraft, prompted the development of expert players who were dealt with like VIPs. These players collected massive fan followings and laid out the possibility that gaming could be a genuine profession way.

The development of E-sports was likewise worked with by the improvement of explicit associations and associations. The development of substances like the Korean e-Sports Affiliation (KeSPA) and the Electronic Games Association (ESL) made organized cutthroat biological systems. These associations normalized rules, gave occasion association, and laid the preparation for an expert E-sports scene.

E-sports and Gaming Society

E-sports' significant effect on gaming society is obvious in different ways. Cutthroat gaming has presented another degree of commitment and yearning to gamers. It has moved the concentration from simple easygoing play to dominating the game and taking a stab at greatness.

Proficient players, frequently alluded to as "geniuses," are respected inside the gaming local area. They act as wellsprings of motivation for hopeful gamers who fantasy about transforming their energy into a vocation. Star players are praised for their expertise, devotion, and the endless hours they put resources into sharpening their art.

The ubiquity of E-sports has additionally filled the development of gaming content on stages like Jerk and YouTube. Gamers and E-sports aficionados make content going from live floods of their interactivity to inside and out investigation and critique. These substance makers have become powerful figures inside the gaming local area, forming the preferences and inclinations of their crowds.

The way of life of E-sports reaches out to in-game beauty care products, frequently alluded to as "skins." These are corrective things that change the presence of in-game characters or weapons. Players can buy or exchange these skins, and some of them have acquired critical worth. The charm of interesting and outwardly striking skins has turned into a piece of gaming society.

E-sports and Music

The connection between E-sports and music is one of shared impact. E-games frequently highlight unrecorded music exhibitions as a feature of their diversion setup. These exhibitions add to the scene of E-games, giving a tangible encounter that reaches out past the gaming rivalry.

Significant craftsmen and groups have performed at E-games, adding to their social importance. These exhibitions are communicated to a huge number of watchers, featuring the standard allure of E-sports. The intermingling of music and E-sports has made interesting social minutes.

Alternately, E-sports has impacted the music business. Game soundtracks, especially those of famous E-sports titles, have created devoted followings. Writers who make music for E-sports titles have earned respect for their commitments to the gaming experience. Music motivated by or made for E-sports has turned into a subgenre by its own doing.

E-sports and Style

The universe of E-sports has stretched out its impact to the domain of style. E-sports associations and groups frequently have their own product, including shirts, hoodies, and other marked attire. Fans gladly wear this product to show their help for their number one groups and players.

Joint efforts between design brands and E-sports associations have become progressively normal. These organizations produce restricted release clothing lines that mix the style of the two universes. Style planners perceive the allure of E-sports to a youthful and various crowd, setting aside it an appealing room for cooperation.

Gaming society has likewise impacted style. Styles that were once viewed as specialty, for example, streetwear and techwear, have acquired more extensive acknowledgment. The lively and outwardly striking plans found in gaming society have advanced into standard design, impacting the feel of apparel and extras.

E-sports and Traditional press

E-sports has changed from a subculture to a standard social peculiarity. Significant media sources and sports networks currently give inclusion of E-games, offering similar degree of consideration and investigation as conventional games. E-sports rivalries, especially those with huge award pools, are presently broadcast, giving them admittance to a more extensive crowd.

The Olympic Games have likewise investigated the incorporation of E-sports as a decoration occasion. While the similarity of E-sports with customary games stays a subject of discussion, the affirmation of E-sports as a potential Olympic discipline is a demonstration of its developing impact.

E-sports have tracked down their position in the realm of narratives and movies. Creations like "The Global" and "Allowed to Play" have given bits of knowledge into the lives and encounters of E-sports experts. These narratives act as social ancient rarities that encapsulate the business.

E-sports and Publicizing

E-sports' thriving notoriety has made it an appealing stage for publicizing and promoting. Large companies have perceived the capability of E-sports as a showcasing direct and have put resources into sponsorships and brand organizations.

Organizations like Intel, Coca-Cola, and Red Bull have become central members in E-sports sponsorship. They adjust their brands to E-sports associations, players, and occasions. These sponsorships have offered monetary help to the business as well as added to the authenticity and social meaning of E-sports.

Publicizing inside E-sports reaches out to in-game promoting, where brands coordinate their items or administrations into the virtual universe of the game. For example, a hustling game might highlight boards advancing certifiable brands, making a powerful type of promoting.

E-sports and Social Acknowledgment

E-sports' excursion from a specialty subculture to a standard social peculiarity has involved conquering generalizations and biases. The possibility of gamers as lowlife, socially disconnected people has given way to a more different and comprehensive portrayal of the gaming local area.

E-sports associations and industry pioneers have been proactive in resolving issues connected with variety and inclusivity. Drives like Ladies in Games and female E-sports groups plan to advance orientation balance in the business. Endeavors have been made to establish a climate that invites people, all things considered.

The LGBTQ+ people group has likewise found a spot in E-sports. E-sports associations and players have pushed for LGBTQ+ freedoms and inclusivity, for certain groups taking part in drives like the You Can Play Task, which advances LGBTQ+ inclusivity in sports.

Worldwide portrayal and the variety of players have additionally improved E-sports' social acknowledgment. Players from everywhere the world partake in E-sports contests, addressing various nations and societies.

7.2 The blurring lines between gaming and mainstream entertainment

The universe of diversion is going through a huge change, with gaming assuming a urgent part in this development. What was once a specialty subculture has turned into a social juggernaut that obscures the lines among gaming and standard diversion. This change is powered by innovative progressions, moving shopper inclinations, and the rising assembly of gaming, film, music, and customary media. In this investigation of the obscuring lines among gaming and standard amusement, we will dive into the elements driving this peculiarity and the effect it has on our way of life.

The Ascent of Intuitive Narrating

One of the most convincing parts of gaming that has added to its reconciliation with standard amusement is intuitive narrating. Computer games have developed from shortsighted accounts to complicated, vivid, and genuinely thunderous encounters. Games like "The Remainder of Us," "Red Dead Reclamation," and "The Witcher 3" have carried realistic narrating to the front of gaming.

These games are not just about ongoing interaction; they are tied in with drawing in players in vivid accounts. Players become dynamic members in the story, pursuing decisions that shape the result. This degree of organization and submersion has drawn matches with conventional narrating mediums, similar to film and TV, which are innately more uninvolved.

The idea of spreading accounts, where players go with decisions that influence the storyline, has turned into a sign of present day gaming. This intuitive component has reclassified the limits of narrating, permitting players to become co-creators of their encounters. In doing as such, gaming has brought another degree of intelligence and commitment that rivals conventional account structures.

Transmedia Narrating

The idea of transmedia narrating has arisen because of this obscuring of lines among gaming and standard amusement. Transmedia narrating includes the development of a story across different media stages. On account of gaming, it frequently implies broadening the story into different types of media, like books, comics, motion pictures, or television series.

A conspicuous illustration of transmedia narrating is "The Witcher" series, which started as a progression of Clean dream books by Andrzej Sapkowski. The outcome of the books prompted the production of computer games and, all the more as of late, a well known Netflix television series. The story, characters, and universe of "The Witcher" have risen above the gaming medium and become piece of standard culture.

Transmedia narrating permits makers to contact a more extensive crowd and give different section focuses into a story. Devotees of the game might be acquainted with the books or television series, while fanatics of the books might become keen on the games. This interconnected narrating approach encourages a feeling of local area among fans and develops their commitment with the story.

The Streaming Insurgency

The rise of live streaming stages, especially Jerk, significantly affects the combination of gaming and standard amusement. Jerk permits gamers to communicate their interactivity progressively, furnishing watchers with the valuable chance to watch, interface with, and support their number one decorations. This live connection has made a feeling of local area and transformed gaming into a passive activity.

Live streaming has advocated gaming as well as obscured the lines among gaming and customary diversion. Big names, performers, and entertainers have joined the stage to associate with fans and take part in gaming content. This hybrid has acquainted a more extensive crowd with gaming society and added to the social meaning of gaming.

Also, live streaming has developed past gaming to envelop different types of amusement, for example, "simply visiting" streams, where decorations connect with their crowd continuously. These streams frequently incorporate conversations, back and forth discussions, and even music exhibitions. The flexibility of live streaming stages has made them a focal center for an extensive variety of diversion content.

Famous people in Gaming

The combination of famous people into the gaming scene is one more sign of the obscuring lines among gaming and standard diversion. Notable figures from music, film, and sports have communicated their affection for gaming and have effectively taken part in gaming occasions and content creation.

Artists like Travis Scott have wandered into the gaming domain by holding virtual shows inside well known games like "Fortnite." These occasions have drawn gigantic crowds and displayed the capability of gaming as a stage for music exhibitions.

Entertainer Keanu Reeves turned into a fan number one in the gaming local area after his appearance in the computer game "Cyberpunk 2077." The hybrid between Reeves' Hollywood notoriety and the gaming scene added to the game's social importance and created colossal fervor.

The association of superstars in gaming occasions and content has overcome any issues among gaming and standard culture. It has made new roads for coordinated effort and opened up open doors for cross-advancement between ventures.

Esports and Conventional Games

Esports, the serious side of gaming, has earned respect as a genuine brandishing pursuit. Significant games establishments, like the Philadelphia 76ers, the New York Yankees, and the Brilliant State Champions, have put resources into esports possession. They perceive the common components of rivalry, being a fan, and cooperation between customary games and esports.

Esports have additionally wandered into conventional games settings, holding live occasions in fields and arenas. This assembly of scenes features the equals between the two universes and shows the social meaning of esports.

Conventional games associations, like the NBA and the NFL, have sent off their own esports associations, further overcoming any barrier between the two areas. The NBA 2K Association and the Irritate NFL Title Series are instances of how customary games associations have expanded their venture into the universe of esports.

The Social Effect of Gamers

The ascent of gaming society is obvious in the developing impact of gamers themselves. Gaming superstars, frequently alluded to as "happy makers" or "powerhouses," have amassed enormous followings on stages like YouTube and Jerk. They have become pioneers, forming the inclinations of their crowds and impacting the social scene.

These substance makers produce an extensive variety of content, from interactivity recordings and surveys to video blogs and webcasts. They have risen above the customary bounds of gaming and become unmistakable figures in amusement, with a making the change to conventional media.

Powerful satisfied makers have even been pursued by distributers and designers to advance their games. These makers can influence general assessment, making them fundamental in molding the outcome of new deliveries.

Social Acknowledgment and Personality

The obscuring lines among gaming and standard diversion have likewise added to a change in social acknowledgment and personality. Gaming is not generally restricted to a specialty subculture; it is an energetic and various piece of our social scene.

E-sports play had a critical impact in testing generalizations and biases related with gaming. Ladies in gaming, for example, have been pushing for more noteworthy portrayal and acknowledgment. Associations and drives like Ladies in Games and female e-sports groups have arisen to advocate for orientation uniformity in the business.

The LGBTQ+ people group has likewise found a spot in gaming and e-sports. The support for LGBTQ+ freedoms and inclusivity has been embraced by e-sports associations and players. A few groups take part in drives like the You Can Play Venture, which advances LGBTQ+ inclusivity in sports.

The incorporation of worldwide players and groups has extended the social variety inside e-sports. Gamers from everywhere the world contend in e-games, addressing various nations and societies. This worldwide reach has made e-sports a more comprehensive and different social space.

The Future of Obscuring Lines

The continuous union of gaming and standard diversion is probably going to proceed, with a few variables molding its direction. Innovation will assume a critical part, especially with the coming of computer generated reality (VR), increased reality (AR), and 5G network. These mechanical headways will open up new roads for vivid amusement encounters that overcome any barrier among gaming and customary media.

The impact of gaming society on style is additionally expected to develop. Styles that were once viewed as specialty, for example, streetwear and techwear, have acquired more extensive acknowledgment. The lively and outwardly striking plans found in gaming society have advanced into standard design, affecting the feel of dress and frill.

Moreover, the connection among gaming and music, as well as the impact of gaming on the music business, is supposed to advance. Music exhibitions at gaming occasions will turn out to be significantly more intricate and vital to the generally social experience. Gaming-enlivened music and the effect of gaming on music creation will probably extend.

7.3 The role of e-sports in redefining what it means to be a "gamer"

Lately, the gaming scene has seen a critical change. What was once a specialty side interest delighted in by a moderately little gathering of lovers has developed into a worldwide social peculiarity. Vital to this advancement is the universe of cutthroat gaming, or e-sports. E-sports, short for electronic games, has re-imagined the manner in which we view computer games as well as the actual personality of the people who draw in with them. In this investigation of the job of e-sports in reclassifying being a "gamer," we will dive into the variables driving this change and its effect on the gaming local area.

The Advancement of Gaming

Gaming has made considerable progress from its initial days when it was principally viewed as a single or, best case scenario, a nearby multiplayer movement. The approach of the web, reasonable rapid associations, and the multiplication of internet gaming networks denoted a defining moment. Gamers could now interface with each other from various regions of the planet, empowering another degree of social collaboration inside gaming.

With online multiplayer games, the idea of the "gamer" started to grow. At this point not restricted to a solitary player experience or nearby companions, gamers could partake in gigantic web-based universes and connect with a different cluster of players. Gaming was as of now not simply a diversion; it was a social movement that cultivated associations and kinships.

Online people group, gatherings, and stages like Jerk and YouTube play had a urgent impact in joining gamers. These stages have permitted gamers to share their encounters, systems, and content, further obscuring the lines of who is thought of as a "gamer." The way of life of gaming was not generally bound to a specialty subculture; it was becoming standard.

E-sports: Cutthroat Gaming as a Passive activity

E-sports arose as a characteristic augmentation of web based gaming, giving a cutthroat outlet to players who planned to succeed in their #1 titles. What separates e-sports from customary gaming is its change into a passive activity. E-games are coordinated, proficient rivalries where top players or groups seek significant monetary rewards and worldwide acknowledgment.

Significant e-sports competitions, like The Worldwide for Dota 2, the Class of Legends Big showdown, and the Overwatch Association Fabulous Finals, draw huge worldwide crowds. These occasions are not generally restricted to the gaming scene; they are standard social exhibitions. They highlight fabulous opening services, unrecorded music exhibitions, and elaborate special visualizations.

The obscuring lines among gaming and standard diversion become especially clear during these competitions. Music shows inside games, superstar appearances, and broadcasting on standard telecom companies all highlight the shift. E-games are presently drawing in watchers who may not distinguish as conventional gamers, augmenting the social allure of gaming.

Changing View of "Gamers"

The ascent of e-sports as a passive activity has fundamentally influenced how gamers are seen. Before, the expression "gamer" frequently conveyed generalizations of people who were disconnected, socially abnormal, or excessively consumed by their side interest. Nonetheless, the perceivability of e-sports and the local area it has cultivated have tested these generalizations.

E-sports experts, frequently alluded to as "star players," have become celebrated figures inside the gaming local area and then some. These players are perceived for their devotion, expertise, and obligation to their picked games. The change in discernment stretches out past the actual players; it envelops the more extensive gaming local area.

Proficient gamers are currently viewed as competitors, committing extended periods to preparing, refining methodologies, and idealizing their abilities. Their accounts of determination, difficult work, and penance have refined the gaming scene, introducing a story that reverberates with a wide crowd. They act as good examples, exemplifying the upsides of discipline and desire.

Also, the association of superstars in e-sports has obscured the lines among gaming and standard culture. Notable figures from music, film, and conventional games have communicated their affection for gaming and effectively partake in e-games and content creation. Their investment has acquainted a more extensive crowd with the gaming local area and added to the social meaning of gaming.

The Professionalization of E-sports

The professionalization of e-sports plays had a significant impact in reclassifying being a "gamer." E-sports associations, associations, and groups have presented a degree of design and association to the cutthroat gaming scene. These substances have normalized rules, gave occasion association, and laid the basis for an expert e-sports climate.

E-sports experts currently partake in thorough preparation regimens, like competitors in conventional games. They are upheld by mentors, administrators, and therapists who assist them with arriving at their max operation. The obligation to greatness and the longing to contend at the most significant level have raised e-sports to a regarded and genuine type of rivalry.

E-sports groups and associations frequently have their own marking, logos, and product. The ascent of these associations has made a feeling of personality and local area inside the gaming scene. Fans enthusiastically support their #1 groups and players, wearing pullovers, going to live occasions, and making a feeling of having a place that rises above geological limits.

This professionalization has stretched out to the business side of e-sports. E-sports associations create income through sponsorships, brand organizations, stock deals, and media freedoms bargains. The monetary progress of e-sports has additionally legitimized the business and prompted more noteworthy acknowledgment of e-sports experts.

Variety and Inclusivity in E-sports

Perhaps of the most eminent change in the gaming local area is the accentuation on variety and inclusivity. E-sports associations and industry pioneers have been proactive in resolving issues connected with orientation, race, and character.

Endeavors to advance variety in e-sports have prompted the production of female e-sports groups and drives like Ladies in Games. These drives mean to increment female portrayal in the business and give amazing open doors to ladies to seek after vocations in e-sports. They challenge the idea that gaming is only a male-overwhelmed space.

The LGBTQ+ people group has additionally found acknowledgment inside e-sports. E-sports associations and players have upheld for LGBTQ+ privileges and inclusivity, for certain groups taking part in drives like the You Can Play Task, which advances LGBTQ+ inclusivity in sports.